THE MOVEMENT

How I got this body by never going to the gym in my life.

Written by Jack Garbarino

The exercises present in this book are to be performed at your own risk. Always consult with your physician before beginning any workout regimen.

CONTENTS

CHAPTER 1   Something that was mine   1

CHAPTER 2   Off the rail I go   7

CHAPTER 3   What you have is yours   17

CHAPTER 4   Backs of photos   27

CHAPTER 5   My attention   39

CHAPTER 6   Basic, super, or premium   63

CHAPTER 7   Short term glory   77

CHAPTER 8   Stay out of the brush   89

CHAPTER 9   Baboons   109

CHAPTER 10   Insurmountable   119

CHAPTER 11   My new team   127

CHAPTER 12   Right half of the board   149

CHAPTER 1

Something that was mine

Steps. Four seemed like fourteen to me. It was hard with legs like mine. Most middle kid students headed to gym class had thin legs. Some had muscles, like, defined muscles. Those were the ones that would torment me fairly soon, straight through to high school. Needless to say, I was that kid. The one fat kid in every school that was unfortunate enough to not have something to make himself stand out from my weight.

Some kids have awesome baseball cards, or a rich parent to brag about me. I was lucky to even have one of those- parents- but she was not rich. Not even enough to purchase baseball cards. All of our money- some kids would say too much of it- went to feeding the two of us. I'll tell you what we had that most children, jungle children, as I'd come to learn, were starved of even more than food.

Fun.

I pulled open the classroom door.

"Hey, Jack Porker," shouted one of the kids. Following the announcement was the typical chorus of students' laughter. At that point, I would normally puff up my round cheeks and shuffle the sandy brown hair from my face. This time, I let it slide. He actually mentioned my first name, so that was a plus. Better to know that I wasn't just a big round ball to them.

"Hi," I said meekly. I shuffled through the not-as-quiet giggling to my seat in the front of the class. And yes, I knew what I was doing.

Setting myself up to be an even bigger target. The fat kid who was also super studious and the teacher's pet. Like with my weight, I refused to defend myself. In actuality, I only sat up front because of my poor vision.

On days like these, when the cold outside caused my breath to fog up my glasses, it was better not to wear them at all. But I was quickly regretting that decision. The teacher, Mr. James, had scripted something onto the chalkboard. To me it read something along the lines of "lawn of motives". I regretted what I did next, but it was too late. My hand was raised.

Another round of laughter resonated through the class. This time my cheeks had puffed up.

"This, Mr. Garbarino, says "laws of motion", not "lawn of motives". I would suggest bringing your glasses from now on," Mr. James said coldly. He wasn't the nicest teacher, but he was the smartest. He knew his sciences. Chemistry. Biology. Anatomy. "I hope you read the homework, because I want you to recite before the class what the first law is. Stand up and say it, please."

The please was unexpected, but even without that addition, I would've stood anyway.

"Newton's first law of motion states that unless an external force acts upon an object, it is at a constant rate of motion, or inertia."

"Very good. You may sit."

And like that, the bullying me portion of class was over. Mr. James, in his trademark labcoat with his initials "M.J." stitched into the breast pocket, resumed to teach us all about movement, how it never truly rests. He called inertia a subjective reference for those who rely on their naked eyes. He said how, even if unseen, inertia only applies to two things: rocks and religion. I never understood the religion part, but he clearly thought it was applicable.

Mr. James explained that even though our bodies may not be moving, as in by our own feet, the insides are always in action. He explained how cell processes perpetually run, how blood does not stop flowing, and how the brain- unless dead- always sends signals to the rest of the body. When one student challenged his assumption, he countered with "Your brain belongs to you, does it not. The brain runs your systems, even without your conscious command. Right now, even in your stupor, it is working hard. Do not interrupt me again."

That was a swifter defeat than most. I guess Mr. James was fed up after our first period class. He never snapped like that before. Anyway, he gave us our assignment. "Read chapter four and be prepared for a quiz on Monday." At least he gave us fair warning.

We all rose and exited the class, most of us heading for the same third period class, the one I dreaded so much. I was hoping that with my poor sight, the teacher would just let me skip out. For once, I was lucky.

I sat there in on the sidelines of the gym, watching all the other boys build up a sweat playing basketball. All of them taller than me, and based off the group of girls watching them on the opposite side of the gym, cuter. They went back and forth in the school jerseys provided us, the gilded lion emblazoned on the backs, below their numbers. With leaps, sprints, and serpentine movements, their arms and legs looked as incredible as they likely felt. With each dunk or lay-up, the girls would cheer. Each almost slip up or brick, I would snort under my breath.

The gym teacher, Mr. Edwards, walked up to me, a soccer ball under his arm. He was more friendly than Mr. James, but just as smart. He was dressed in his Friday referee outfit, a tradition he made back before I started to attend Lowen Middle School. It was complete with the whistle he had draped round his neck.

"Hey, Jack, how you doing?" he said softly.

"I'm fine," I responded. "I'm sorry I forgot my glasses."

"Are you?"

I suddenly felt guilty. I was hoping he wouldn't see through my plan, but the fact was that Mr. Edwards was smart in very different sense than Mr. James. Mr. Edwards was great at picking up on little subtleties, and mine were an open book today.

"What do you mean?" I said to try and disarm the speech I felt coming on. My luck had officially run out.

"You've been sitting here mocking them this entire hour. Instead, you should be playing with them," he told me with a stern look on his face.

"But they'll just call me Porker and then refuse to pass me the ball."

"Then take the ball from them. It's a legitimate part of basketball. If you don't have the ball, simply take it."

"But I'm not fast like any of them." I pointed out at the court and Mr. Edwards followed my finger. The center for our basketball team, Harrison Legend, leaped above the other boys and ripped the ball out of the air like it had hands on it. He stomped down on the court with his size eleven feet and went right back up for a quick lay-up. By the way he was celebrating with chest slaps and roaring, he had secured victory for his team. They all swarmed him and lifted up both of his arms. Neither were particularly big, but they were definitely toned. Fully erect, they looked like spaghetti strands with pieces of burger meat to simulate the grooves of muscle of his forearms and biceps.

"Or strong," I finally said.

"Then get faster and stronger. It may sound hard to you, but you just haven't found your way yet. Once you start trying, it'll hit you," he paused and snapped, "like that."

With the ring of the bell, the most painful half of the day was over. It was time for my favorite part of school: lunch.

The line was always short in the school's basement cafeteria. This lunch room was reserved for students with good grade point averages. I was horrified to learn that this semester, a few of my tormentors proved to be buckling down on their studies. I saw their predatory eyes set on me as they waited just beyond the end of line, trays of food in their hands. I put them out of my mind and focused on the food. That was something that didn't take much work.

The menu for Friday was as typical as me hating gym, or Mr. James' labcoat. It was pizza day, but our school was more well funded than most, so we had actual pizza, and not those bagels with cheese and pepperoni spread all over them. I grabbed two slices- wanted a third- of pepperoni, a carton of chocolate milk, and a brownie. With a portion of heaven in my hands, I headed for what was going to be hell.

"Hey, Porker," taunted one of the boys still clad in his jersey. He had the same kind of hair as me, but his eyes were small and dark, like those of a rat.

"You sure you need that second slice?" teased the one to the right. He had red hair and a small collection of freckles using the real estate over his nose.

"My guess is he needs to eat his own body weight in food every day just to survive," remarked Harrison. Guess he was paying more attention in biology. We had just covered the section talking about animal diets. Most predators at the top of their respective food chains would require a large amount of food per day. The only thing wrong here was that I wasn't at the top of the food chain. I was at the very bottom, possibly even lower than the chess club/comic book nerds.

"Just leave me alone." That was my only defense. I wasn't confrontational, and I wasn't witty enough for three comebacks. It would only lead to more back and forths, and my insults weren't going to be a fraction as good as theirs would. I sluggishly walked around them, nearly tripping over my own feet in my haste.

I reached my favorite table in the western corner. It was right below one of the speakers. The corner was structured so that any sounds that rose from its direction would not pierce my ears. So when the harsh sound of bell rang, marking the end of lunch, I would only half hear it. But until then, I once more turned back to my food. I grabbed both slices of pizza, rolled them into one another, and bit down. My own invention, a pizza-wrapped pizza burrito. In between bites, I sipped my chocolate milk. I saved the brownie as a pick-me-up just in case the student teasing became too unbearable.

The rest of the day was surprisingly easy. Preceding the bell at lunch's end, there was an announcement of a field trip on Monday to a museum of historic art. Everyone only talked of that and I was able to coast through math, English, and free period peacefully. The even better news, I could save my brownie for the bus ride home.

I dressed for the warmth in my black and green winter coat, puffy with air, a pair of green earmuffs, and an emerald scarf with midnight stripes. Despite all the blubber jokes tossed at me, I was not going to suffer from frostbite. I could not stand the cold any more than I could running laps at the beginning of gym.

I was happy to be relinquished of that horror one more day, thanks to the field trip. The permission slips they handed out came with a poster. The front was decorated with images of the things they had on display, from statues of gladiators to paintings like the Mona Lisa.

With the high fields of snow at the sides of the walkway, what happened next came as an utter shock. Suddenly, and from both sides, I was pelted by deeply packed snowballs. I yelped as I raised my hands to shield my face. It did little good. Someone out of all my assailants was making tiny snowballs, and they all pierced my flimsy shield. I turned and ran, the snowballs unceasing. I turned just enough to see the bus pulling up. I ran inside of it, still being pelted, when:

"Hey, knock it off!" the bus driver yelled at whomever was behind the assault. I was confident it was to be at my defense, but then she yelled "You're getting water on the steps! Stop it!"

Even though it wasn't solely for my benefit, I was happy when the onslaught was over. Not just for today, but my week was over. For two days, I was now free of the torment and mocking tendencies of Harrison and his buddies. For two days, it was just me and my buddy, Steve Jobs.

CHAPTER 2
Off the rail I go

After warming up at home, snuggled under my bed sheets, I pulled out my science textbook and commenced reading the chapter as assigned. This one was about the laws of motion as well, but it went into more detail than Mr. James had earlier. It applied those rules to the usefulness of the six simple machines: levers, pulleys, wedges, inclined planes, screws, and wheels and axles.

It said how levers were the external forces that initiated movement in something. The rate at which that object moved was affected by the pulleys and inclined planes. Whether they slowed or increased the speed of the object depended on how they were used. For example, a car going up an inclined plane (expressway exit) is immediately slowed upon contact with it. However, the force of a pulley, or the elastic force of a rubber band could propel an object much faster than its normal means.

Wedges, screws, and wheels were the instruments that secured the levers, pulleys, and planes. For the elastic of a rubber band to be stretched, a wedge must be applied to one of its ends, like a finger. Screws and wheels are perfect for keeping levers and other such gear controls in place and in proper order.

I took notes on all of it and jotted down every last detail I thought might be pertinent. I was going to be ready for my quiz on Mon...oh, wait. The field trip was Monday. That meant I was going to either be excused, or have an extra day to study. I was suddenly more thrilled about this weekend now that I could study a little less.

When the doorbell, rang, I practically shot down the stairs. And yes, Steve was a good enough friend that my excitement outweighed my hatred for running. I shouted at my mother that I would answer the door. She didn't respond, so she was probably out back. She didn't have much of a garden, but that didn't stop her from trying to build one.

I yanked the door wide open and to my surprise, Steve wasn't there. It was his mother. She usually waited at the car while he entered.

"Hi, Mrs. Jobs," I said, slightly unnerved. "Where's Steve?" I tried to peek around her, but our doorway was too skinny, so I couldn't get a look at the car.

"He's back at home. He needs to finish his homework before he can play, so I came to pick you up without him. He should be done by the time we get there," she said so gingerly. She was always sweet to me. Never a harsh word, or comment about my weight with her. I truly wish that my classmates would adopt her attitude. She peered at me with her warm eyes, so vibrant and full of light. It was almost like when my mom would console me about the bullies. But still, I felt a sense of dread washing over me. I was going to find out why pretty soon.

I was in the front seat, seat buckled after a stern reminder from Mrs. Jobs. I never really liked seatbelts. The strap was uncomfortable and choking, but I endured. Mrs. Jobs offered to stop at nearly every fast food place we crossed on the way to her home, but I kindly refused. The brownie I ate on the bus was good enough for the time being. It took some time, but I realized that she was only trying to buy time for Steve to finish his homework. Her frantic, every-ten-second glances at her watch gave her away. When she offered to buy me something from McDonalds, I finally consented.

"So, how're things at school, Jack?" she asked, then wiped her mouth of grease and ketchup.

"They're going fine. I'm still holding steady at a 3.2 GPA. My mom says that if I get a 4.0, that she'll take me to a five star restaurant for my birthday," I explained. I guess I was hungry after all. I bit into my cheeseburger and my stomach immediately bellowed its approval.

"That's good. A young man working hard should always be rewarded. However..." she trailed off and then sipped her drink.

"What is it?" I asked, feeling another speech on the horizon.

The muscle in her jaw moved back and forth and she looked as if contemplating speaking up. When she sighed, I knew it was coming. "Jack, I know your mother loves you, and I do, too. But..." she sucked in a breath. "But, I think you should try eating a little healthier. It's fine if you want to eat often, but perhaps try substituting some of the sweets for vegetables."

"I eat vegetables," I said defensively.

"What did you have for lunch today?" Her voice had lost its warmth and replaced it with a touch of condescension. Or was the word compassion? Back then, I could not exactly tell the two apart with most people. Steve was always clear to me, but his mother surely wasn't.

"I ate two slices of pizza, a brownie...and a carton of chocolate milk," I said. I looked up anticipating to see a smug look on her face, but it was more sympathetic. Guess she was going down the compassion route. "But there were vegetables on the pizza," I stated. "Olives, mushrooms, and peppers."

She shook her head. "Jack, you need more than that. I want you to promise me something, ok?" I felt I had no other choice than to nod, so I did. "I want you to eat three fruits and vegetables every day, from now on. Can you do that?" I nodded again. "But, I want you to understand something. Those six fruits and vegetables are to each one thing you would usually eat throughout the day. One less pizza slice in exchange for one more piece of broccoli. Do you understand?"

"Does it have to be broccoli?" I asked, which seemed to amuse her.

"No. It can be any vegetable. Oh, and while we're on the subject... how do you feel about carrots?"

The answer to that question was a huge, fat, "These are delicious!" I exclaimed. I bit into the carrot stick once again and chewed away. It was like biting into a solid, but brittle piece of orange chalk, but it tasted way better. I couldn't really identify the taste- my palate was small- but it was like this bittersweet stick. I reached into the bag and pulled out a handful of them. Mrs. Jobs gave me a sheet of paper towel to hold them in as I ate.

We were in her living room, waiting on Steve to make his appearance. We had arrived only minutes ago, but the wait was killing me. It

and these carrots. I wished broccoli tasted this good. We were perched
on their long, white leather couch. It was slippery beneath my round
cheeks- not the ones that puff up- but the pillows behind me were soft
as marshmallows against my aching back. I was not going to sit in
Mrs. Jobs's front seat again.

"So, how much homework did they give him? It's almost 5:30," I
said. I was losing patience. I wanted my best friend now. I wanted us
to go to his room to play videogames and read through his comics.
But lately, reading comics was being replaced by fidgeting around with
the electronics in his room. He was developing this sort of engineer
side to him, and it was even cooler than comics.

"It should be over soon." She looked down at my paper towel.
"Would you like more carrots?" I nodded. She grabbed the towel from
me and went back to the kitchen.

I leaned back and nestled deeper into the pillow. I heard the sound
of dress shoes tapping on marble and turned to my right. I looked and
saw Steve descending the stairs with his father and three other men.
The three men were all dressed in the same suit. Like Mr. James, there
was something written on their breast pockets. I believe the initials
were "D.J.H." I was certain that the J and H stood for Junior High, but
the D was new to me...wait, no, it was a C. I got a better look as they
reached the ground floor and then crossed to the front door. "C.J.H."?
I wasn't sure what that was, but I'd never heard of a school with those
initials.

Steve and his father, Mr. Jobs, bade farewell to the men and then
closed the door. Mrs. Jobs joined them at the door and she whispered
to both of them. When she whispered to Steve, she pointed in my
direction. He whirled with the biggest smile on his face. And like that,
I'd forgotten all about the carrots, the quiz, the field trip, everything.
I'd see that smile again, and not just on him. In my future, the jungle
children would be giving me that same smile. I would love, as I loved
this one that Steve was giving me.

Steve grabbed my arm and dragged right back up his marble stair-
case. We raced through the hallway on the second floor and stopped
before the second door on the left. The first was to the bathroom. Steve
opened his door and we scrambled inside before shutting the door
tight. I turned and smiled. Steve's room looked just it always did in

recent weeks.

There were broken open pieces of technology all over the floor, from radios to VCRs and more. His tv looked intact on his bedside mantle, but I was sure that parts of it were already gone, so I made no move to turn it on. He pulled out a thin, black box from under his bed. It was adorned with plastic latches on the front. He flipped the hatches and revealed the collection of tools inside, from screwdrivers to hammers to nails and a small mallet. I wasn't sure that was a tool, but it could be used that way, too, I'm positive. We were no doubt about to tinker with something, but something was nagging at me, and I had to let it out.

"So, what were those people here for?" I asked.

"They came and tested me, that's all," Steve said, but he shuddered before answering.

"Test for what? Don't you always get 4.0s?"

"That's why the testers came." He dropped the toolbox and then shifted to face me directly. "My parents wanted me to keep it a secret until the results came next Friday, but I'm sure it's fine to tell you." It wouldn't be. Steve sighed and then spoke up again. "The school suggested that I take a test to see if I can bump up two full grades," he said in a haste to jumble up his words.

"My, my, Steve Jobs. That's great. Then we'd both be in seventh grade. It'd be awesome," I said cheerfully. "Are you gonna come to Lowen with me?"

He inhaled so sharply that if his breath were a blade, I would've been decapitated when he said "No."

"Oh, then where will you be going? To that, um, C.J.H.?"

"Yeah, it's called Cupertino Junior High. It's in Cupertino, California."

This time I sucked in a breath. "Is Cupertino nearby?" He shook his head I nearly felt like I was going to chop my own head off. This was my only friend, and he was preparing to go to another school. In a city nowhere near where my mother and I resided. It was already bad enough to have to withstand, but to spend my weekends without my best friend...it would be worse than anything. I choked back tears and instead I smiled. I knew he was getting in. With his grades, he was set to get in anywhere.

"Congratulations," I managed to say between muted sobs. I turned my head and then swallowed. I had to fight off all tears before I faced Steve again. I did it fairly quickly and then we resumed our talk. "When will you leave?"

"Well, if I get in, I will start there in September, so after this semester, we plan to move on out there. I think my parents said shortly after summer comes." Steve spoke of his leaving now more easily. I guess we both just needed a second or two to brace ourselves. And now that I knew he wasn't leaving immediately, that gave me some sort of peace.

"Oh, before I forget, wanna grab some of those carrot sticks?"

He smiled and we ran right out the door.

It turned out I was wrong about the television. He hadn't tinkered in it at all yet. We sat back and watched a bit of cartoons, munching on the carrots like they were popcorn. After that, we moved onto video games. It was cool that we got in some more time to play Super Mario Bros. while Steve's parents and my mother discussed grown up things on the first floor. After about twenty minutes they granted us out of sheer kindness, they said that it was time for Steve to go to bed. My mother and I obliged, thanked them for having me over, and then we went home. I knew I would be seeing Steve again tomorrow. It was Saturday, and that meant one thing: the park.

Saturday was not as chilly as yesterday, but the wind was making up for the week. The cold had been bearable mainly due to low winds, but today was its time for vengeance. And honestly, it shouldn't be this cold in California, but weirder things have happened. Steve and I walked over to the skating rink, one of the few in the city, and were ready to ice skate. I'm not very good, so I hug the edge of the rink. Steve was, compared to me, a gold medalist skater. He could spin and somewhat skate backwards. All the tricks were, in varying degrees, under his belt. My trick: stick to the wall, you won't fall.

I was probably the only one on the rink not adroit in the ice skating craft. And I was okay with that. Unlike at school, I didn't feel the need to hide myself here. These people could whisper about me all the wanted. Nothing the said would be repeated the very next day at the very same time.

I rounded the rink one full time. It took around fifteen minutes. Once I did, I spotted the worst of faces. And here, of all places. Was someone trying to ruin my day with Steve? It sure seemed like it.

Harrison and a couple of his teammates strolled on over to rent some skates. I took advantage of the exit right next to me and vacated the rink just as they got on. I was hoping to not let Steve in on my nickname. Speak of the devil, he snuck up on me and laid a hand on my shoulder. I actually screamed since I was so on edge.

Steve and a few nearby people jumped at my alarm. I quickly peered over my shoulder and saw that Harrison and his goons hadn't paid my outburst any mind. I took a sigh of relief and faced Steve.

"Don't sneak up on me like that," I said in a ragged tone.

"I didn't sneak up on you. I was calling your name, but you were ignoring me. You kept staring at," he stepped around me and pointed, "at those guys. If they're friends, we should call them over." I didn't register what Steve said until he had already cupped his hands around his mouth. "Hey, you guys in the red hats! Hey!"

And with that, the apocalypse was upon us.

Harrison and his crew had surrounded us near the southeastern part of the rink. This portion was cut off from the other skaters' vision by a rounded out wall. They had on red hats, each with the same insignia as their jerseys, the Lowen Lion. It was a red beast with a grey outline and mane.

"Porker, you know how to skate?" Harrison asked, a bit of shock in his tone.

"Of course," I said, trying to make this as painless as possible.

"You do?" Steve asked with an incredulous expression. His inquiry single-handedly ruined my charade. I could tell by the smile on Harrison's face that he knew I was lying.

"So what if I don't know how to skate," I stated. "I could still beat you in a race!" That there, that was just preteen angst rearing its ugly head at the wrong time.

"Oh?" Harrison lifted one eyebrow. "Wanna bet?"

"Jack, let's just go. We don't have to listen to him." Steve grabbed my arm and tried to pull me away, but this time, I was not backing down. I couldn't let Harrison and his stooges take this away from me. This spot was always just for me to enjoy with my best friend. I was not going to let him soil this spot, too.

"Name your price," I said stubbornly.

"The race will be to see who can round the rink three times first. The loser has to get a name of the winner's choice stamped on their forehead, and they have to wear it for the entire field trip on Monday," Harrison said. He extended his hand. "Do we have a deal?"

"And it can be any name?" I had one in mind, but I needed to be sure of the terms. Harrison nodded. "Then we have a deal." I shook his hand.

"Jack," Steve mumbled worriedly.

"Don't worry, Steve. I'll win for sure."

We both stood at the entrance of the rink, poised to begin at a pen's drop. I was clung to the rail and he was shifting his legs anxiously. His legs seemed steady and strong, but nimble was another thing. They shifting soon came to to be perceived by me as wobbling. I guess there was a reason I'd never seen him here before- he had never skated. So, I had some sort of edge here. But to take full advantage, I had to release the rail. And yes, by breaking my rule, I would fall, but so would he.

One of Harrison's friends shouted go and the race had begun. AS expected, Harrison took an early- albeit short- lead. He looked like a spider trying to avoid heat on a hot plate, skittering about trying to gain some sort of foothold. Anywhere. I, on the other hand, had to force myself to go much slower. My jeans were eating away at my thighs, closely positioned together. The chafing was unreal. I had a much better center of gravity, thanks to my height in proportion to me girth, so I didn't have as much trouble securing my footing as Harrison, but his acceleration was definitely out of my reach.

He was already three-fourths around the entire rink and I was only on the first corner stretch. I needed to pick up the pace. I apologized to my already sore thighs and began to push off stronger. Right. Left. Right. Left. I fell. I couldn't stand because the ice was slippery in this one part. One of the security guards who tend to the inexperienced customers slowly approached and helped me to my feet. I looked past him and to the exit and saw that Harrison was getting off the rink.

"But the bet's not over," I whispered.

"C'mon, kid. We've got to let the zamboni freshen up the rink's surface," the guard said curtly. He held my hand and led me over to the exit. I clumsily traipsed on over to Harrison and Steve and the others.

Harrison looked calm and composed, as if he hadn't really struggled at all out there. Guess that's the privilege of being an athlete grants you- the ability of good breathing. I, however, was heaving and gasping like a madman. The guard may have taken care of me, but his pace was too fast to handle, even though I didn't have much work to do. That combined with the heart-pounding race I just tried to win was too stressful on my fat. I'd call them muscles, but I'm not gonna even attempt to fool myself there.

"So, do you wanna continue the bet?" Harrison asked.

I couldn't tell if he was just trying to get me to say no so he could tease me about be a chicken, too, or if he really wanted to call it off. Either way, I was said "Yes."

Steve put up a hand before Harrison and pulled me to the side for a quick intervention. "Jack, you barely managed when the ice was dry. When that zamboni," he pointed toward the machine waxing the ice along the rink's edge, "is done, you won't be able to stand any easier. The friction may be lessened, but that surface of that ice will also be much less likely to allow to stop or navigate accurately as before. If *you* start to fall, you won't be able to recover at all."

"Doesn't matter. I'm still gonna win," I boasted. Steve was usually right about things like that, but I couldn't let his comments get inside my head. I had a race to win...somehow.

The guy on the zamboni vacated the rink some ten minutes later. In that entire team, Steve hadn't stopped trying to convince me to quit the bet. For all his reasons: the ice will be too slippery, my legs would give out under me, or the fact that Harrison was simply faster, it was all futile. I stepped into the rink behind Harrison and saw the newly wiped down ice. It grabbed the rail and slowly inched on over to where I was when the zamboni came on. Harrison and I agreed to resume the race at our last known spots instead of starting over, which meant I was still one lap behind.

I didn't hear anyone shout "start" so my only warning was Harrison passing by me with a huge grin on his face. I released the rail and continued chafing my thighs. I grated them against one another harder and faster than before. But it still wasn't nearly enough. And with my hastened breathing against the chilly air, my glasses- I wore them today- began to fog up, obscuring what little vision I had amidst the other skaters. I didn't even see Harrison pass me a third time. I had myself just finished my first lap.

I knew long beforehand that Harrison had won the bet, but I was at least going to finish my three laps. I withdrew and soared toward the rail several times before I was finally done. When I reached the rail, Harrison and his posse had vanished, but there stood Steve, clapping. I smiled.

Steve helped me on over to a bench and we sat. He filled me in on where Harrison had gone.

"He said he couldn't wait and watch you any longer, so he and his friends returned their skates and left together. But he said he'd have your stamp ready on Monday," Steve relayed to me. "If you ask me, you did really well, though."

"Thanks." I sat back and tried to catch my breath. It would take a while, so I continued the conversation anyway. "I really thought I could beat him."

"I know."

"I would've been able to brag to him for once. And during a field trip. No one was like to stop talking about it anytime soon. I would've stopped being "Porker" for a little while," I said, breathing raggedly through the whole speech.

"You don't have to beat him, Jack. You're better than him. He just wants you to feel like you aren't." Steve stood up and looked around. I didn't bother to follow his eyes to see what drew his attention. "Hey, my mom's here. Guess it's three already. Ready to go home?"

I shook my head. "But I'll go anyway," I said. Just because I was having a bad day was no reason to be rude to Mrs. Jobs. I marched behind Steve to his mom's car. He offered me the front seat, but I immediately turned it down. No way was I going to let him stick me there after that race. We climbed into the car and his mom greeted us warmly.

"How was skating?" she asked sweetly.

CHAPTER 3

What you have is yours

The rest of the weekend was pretty slow after that, but I was glad to let it be slow for two reasons. One was simply to prolong the upcoming verbal stings during the field trip. The other was because I had gone as fast as I wanted to last the entire week, which meant "accidentally" leaving my glasses each day.

After skating on Saturday, Mrs. Jobs drove me home. I undressed from my outer wear and put on pajamas. I stayed in bed, eating some potato chips and watched a few cartoons, mainly Looney Tunes.

My mother was at work until 5pm, so when she came home, I joined her in the living room. I helped her put away the groceries and was pleased to see she had bought a bag of those carrot sticks like I asked. I planned on following Mrs. Jobs's advice, but I was gonna take it slow. Start with carrots and then try the more "green" veggies over time.

My mom brought home some movie choices from BlockBuster, but I was more focused on what to eat for dinner. Primarily, I had to choose what to substitute the carrots with. My mother had brought us chicken, bacon, milk, cereal, bread, pasta, eggs, cheese, peanut butter, jelly, etc. I decided that I'd forfeit the pasta for now. We had grilled chicken with melted cheese on top, bread and carrot sticks as sides, and lemonade to drink. We loved it so much that we ate the same thing for dinner on Sunday, too.

Steve was busy on Sunday with some homework his parents discovered that he'd lied about, so I couldn't hang out with him. And my mother was at work today, too. This was my first Sunday alone in a long while. I had no idea what I was going to do. I sat in bed, watching tv and eating the last of my potato chips. That soon grew boring. I stripped out of my pajamas and put on the same clothes I skated in. I was heading to the backyard when I decided to stop at the bathroom.

It was a rather modest room. We had a simple shower curtain, no designs on it. The floor and walls were tiled, but were white. The toilet was fairly sized, as well as the sink. In the rear of the bathroom, standing just beneath the window, was our scale. I hadn't ever liked that machine, but I was curious. Maybe the carrots were having an affect on me already. I mean, I did all that high-speed skating, so there was a chance my pounds were cut a bit. My last recorded weight was 164 lbs. When both my feet were planted down on the scale, the screen displayed 171 lbs.

"What?!" I couldn't contain my surprise.

Mrs. Jobs said that the carrots would alleviate some of my weight issues. I don't believe this. I ate all those stupid orange pieces of chalk for no reason. And she'd fed me that lie with such a sincere look on her face. Come to think of it, everyone seemed to share that look when they tried to appease me. Mr. Edwards when he said all I needed to do was get stronger and faster. Mrs. Jobs when she told me about fruits and vegetables. And worst of all was Steve, when he assured me that I was better than Harrison. He wasn't even specific as to how Harrison was inferior to me. The vagueness of his encouraging words was enough to make me furious.

The only person lately proving true to their words with their facial expressions was Harrison. Well, his posse, too, but he was the face I saw every time someone called me Porker. He was a symbol of that name, I guess. I don't know if it originated with him or not, but he was someone I felt made the name sting worse than anyone else. Maybe because he was the one that I wished I could be out of everyone I knew. He was smart, athletic, had the girls fawning for him. His life seemed perfect in my eyes. Wherever he was headed, I wanted to get there first. Last. Only. He'd revelled in that life too long, if you ask me.

I stormed out of the bathroom, sick of having that cursed machine in my presence. I continued down the hallway until I reached our back door. I grabbed hold of the doorknob, but it felt chilly to the bones in my hands. If I remembered correctly from anatomy class, they were phalonges or phalanges. One of those. Whatever they were, the cold struck them like a hot knife through snow. I know the expression calls for butter, but I was sick of thinking of food and the cold made the reference valid.

The garden was actually thawing nicely in the afternoon heat. The temperature in California was seeming to return to normal. The intense snowfall was rare and I doubt we'd get this ever again. Now the Sun was returning from its vacation. Wonder what it was like where it went?

My mother's plants were still not blooming, but with the recent cold, it was a blessing that they hadn't wilted at all. Guess they must be doing something right. Probably has something to do with the movement inside of their bodies, as M. James would explain if he were here. The cell processes in constant action on the inside must be working overtime to keep their shells alive and well. I wish mine would act as good. If they worked so hard, then maybe my rotund figure wouldn't exist.

Ok, guess it didn't matter, I was always going to go back to my weight. Somewhere in the back of my head, my brain was controlling a targeting system that always seemed to zero in on that topic. Wherever in my brain it was stored, it was under attack. The only way to shut down the unfriendly fire was to take a nap. Both sides would be forced to rest then. Or so I thought.

Dreams are nasty things sometimes. And I don't mean nightmares, dreams. Nightmares deliberately show you the worst things, based on how your mind perceives them. Dreams though, they have access to the positive perceptions one possesses. For me, all those were things I was trying to drown out on this Sunday afternoon. Food, scales, carrots, Steve. I just wanted a nice, soundless sleep. Now I was going to add dreamless for the next time I decided to nap.

All that happened in the dream was just a repetitive cycling of carrot sticks, scales, and brownies (other foods, too). I stood in the middle, always directly in the middle, no matter how I chose to move, no matter which direction I turned. It was as if I was Earth and the food and scales floating around me had gotten trapped in my orbit. I couldn't understand why, but I began to run, and since it was a dream, I could run for hours without stopping. My orbiting objects stayed with me the entire time. I remembered that I paused and stood, still in full control of my breathing. It was like I hadn't been running at all.

I turned my head up at the alarming sound of clapping. Standing just outside of my orbit was Steve, clapping the same way he had after I finished my three laps. His smile was replaced by a scowl. I couldn't tell if it was mocking applause or if he had just simply tore off the mask he wore in real life. Suddenly, he began to levitate away from me, like we were polar opposites. I gave chase, but now my normal breathing was back and I couldn't keep up with him for long.

I huddled over and sat cross-legged on what I guessed was the ground. The air around me was all dark, save for the immediate area that was illuminated somewhat by an unknown light source. The orbiting items had hovered over closer to me, within reach. I lifted my left hand to grab at one of the brownies, but it shifted over and I almost grabbed a carrot stick instead. I withdrew my hand with a hiss, as if the carrot was a cursed object, something to be wary of. I would not go near them again. I turned, trying my darndest to grab the brownie, but it and the carrots were relentless. Too hungry and tired to continue this farce, I grabbed the carrot stick, all of them that were circling me, and ate them, crunching loudly with every bite.

I woke with a slow start. I batted my eyes apart several dozen times before I confirmed I was no longer dreaming. I managed to roll over onto my back. I scratched my head and then just stared up at my blank, white ceiling. I started to recall all the things that had happened this weekend. The bet, the news about Steve, the field trip. All three were, deep down, bad news for me. But, I needed a way to remember all of them. Those three events, I realized in my later years, were pretty critical to the choices I would soon come to make. And some choices I'm making even now.

Why did I need to remember them? Well, for Steve, I wasn't sure if we'd be able to keep contact, and I wanted to remember my best friend. As for the bet, it was the first time I'd stepped up and confronted Harrison, or anyone, for talking down to me. The field trip, well, that's getting ahead of things.

I played my way through Super Mario Bros. and read up more on the chapter Mr. James had assigned to us. I only had one more day after this one to study, and I felt like I wasn't going to be in the mood tomorrow. I thought more about the six simple machines. How could cells make use of these devices? Were the parts of the body that acted just like them? I didn't have my anatomy textbook from last semester anymore, so I was uncertain. I'd try and see if Mr. James would lend it to me after the quiz.

After long, my mother returned home and we had the same dinner as last night. I'd decided to continue with the carrots, at least until Steve and his parents had officially moved away. I wasn't going to dwell on my absent best friend each time I saw a carrot stick after that, so I decided now that it would be better to stick with that declaration.

We nestled together on the same couch as yesterday, but we watched different movies. In the marathon of black-and-white country flicks like *High Noon* and others, we both fell under sleep's spell. I was thankful that I was able to enjoy my night's rest without a dream.

"Stand still," Harrison barked at me. He grabbed my rounded cheeks, puffed as they were, and held my face still for me. It was like I was a tender-headed little boy getting a haircut. He held me there as his buddies finished writing- you guessed it- Porker on my forehead. When he released me, I rushed to the restroom mirror and gasped at the awful penmanship used to mark my day's shame. Porker had been scribbled across my brow with the finesse of a three fingered child with horrible carpal tunnel. Even with my glasses, it resembled something like "punked".

"What do you think?" Harrison asked mockingly.

"I hope that was rhetorical," I retorted.

"Rhetorical?" he asked, stumped for an answer.

I sighed and walked away. Clearly, his grade point average was heavily influenced by his gym class grade. I heard him and his buddies cackling like hyenas at their artwork, if you were brave enough to call it that.

I was thankful to be sitting in the front this time. Even though everyone had glimpsed the stamp, not everyone could read it. I was even more thankful for that than anything. I grabbed a seat in the front of the bus as soon as I could, right beside the chaperones, but neither of which was my mother. If she heard the laughter right now, she'd only raise a fuss. The other parents turned a blind eye to my torment.

That was a fairly common thing amongst adults, some of them anyway. And it wasn't just that way here in America. Across seas, spanning each of the six habitable continents, children, oriental children, jungle children, etc, they were suffering from these same burdens. I'd never stoop to be the kind of adult that they are. I'd be the kind to be accepted, to be loved and respected.

My mom had packed me a lunch for the trip and I was eager to see what was inside, but she made me promise not to check until it was time to eat. I had thought that she maybe she threw in an extra one or two brownies as she did on my first day of the school year, but that was going to break our tradition. After that, I suspected it of being the carrot sticks, but she wouldn't be that predictable. Perhaps she included a second Caprisun juice box, or a small bag of peanuts. My mouth was watering just from the prospect of those ideas.

We filed out of the bus and the chaperones had placed us into groups. The museum had instructed the school that they could only handle about five students per tour, so the groups would be assigned based on your spot in line. Unfortunately, with my front spot on the bus, and Harrison's quick feet, we were going to be paired together. We both turned and glared at each other upon that simultaneous realization.

Our group was first. A young man in a navy blue polo shirt and black dress pants greeted us in the foyer with a welcoming smile. I felt at ease with him already. I could tell he meant the smile he was giving us. I didn't want to sour our tor, so I pulled my cap down over the "punked" message scribbled just above my eyes. He gathered us in closer, which was spoiling the mood- being closer to Harrison- so I tried my best to ignore his presence.

The young man introduced himself to us. "My name's Lawrence Peters, but you can call me Petey." He led us out of the foyer and under an archway that held a banner with the word "Rome" written across it in dazzling red calligraphy. "And welcome to our ancient Rome exhibit." He swept his hand around and we all took a hard look at the scenery. "We'll be here for about ten minutes, so take the time to look around."

There were several statues of Roman gladiators, a few tomes with historical records, and weaponry from the era laid out in display cases from the ground floor and on the walls to the topmost floor. I could spy around fifteen or so. We all split off to examine what most drew our eyes. For me, it was one of the gladiator statues. This one was chiseled out of some kind of marble stone, but was adorned with what I guessed was a man-made replica of the armor they wore back then. If it was authentic, then good for the museum. Meant they had the funds to acquire such rare items to casually put on display for middle schoolers.

I got as close to the statue as I could without crossing the barrier erected by the four poles and velvet ropes. I awed at the cape, the armor, and the muscles so expertly sculpted. In my wildest dreams would I ever possess muscles of that magnitude. Not to mention that the spear in the statue's hand was likely heavier than it looked, skinny as it was. I couldn't throw that now I had five other versions of myself to help out, and that's without even knowing the proper form to throw the spear. This is the type of person that Harrison would be. Me, I'd be his servant. His "Porker". Even in this period.

I must've spoken that last few thoughts out loud without realizing it, because afterward came "You're too hard on yourself." I turned and saw Petey, the tour guide, approaching me from my left- my good side.

"I wish I was hard on myself," I countered, lying. I was comfortable with my life. It was everyone else who had the issues.

"Then I guess that young man breaking the rules and touching the glass cases over the assortment of knives *isn't* Harrison," Petey said. He nodded beyond me. I turned and saw Harrison doing just what he described.

"Shouldn't you go stop him?" I asked. I blinked when I turned back to Harrison. I knew he wasn't as sharp as I was, but he seemed smarter than to just blatantly break the rules like that. I was hoping this would teach him a lesson.

"Oh, he's on camera. In a few minutes, if he doesn't change his behavior, security will take action," Petey said, but it was oddly in that same welcoming tone he addressed us with moments ago. Strange.

At least I knew Harrison well enough that he would not grow bored of touching the knives anytime soon. He could entertain a thought for ages. Just to give you a sense, I've been Porker since about third grade.

"So, why do you compare yourself with him so much?" Petey's voice was the same degree of warm as before, but the question felt like an all too powerful ice cream headache had suddenly and fiercely afflicted me. I shook my head in response. "Don't want to talk about it. Fair enough." I foolishly hoped that was the end of the conversation. "You know," he started, "gladiators aren't as great as most people would believe them to be. Strong and dutiful soldiers- some, but most did nothing besides follow the orders of another."

"Another? Another gladiator?" That didn't make sense. Unless one of the gladiators was placed in charge of the others, like the general of some great army. Which, I guess, they technically were at some point through history.

"They were led, instructed, and ordered around by a rather enigmatic, hedonistic dictator that would sit around most of each day being bathed and serviced by many that he would barely appreciate if not for the fact they did those things for him, but even then it wasn't expected.

And you know what, the dictator usually enjoyed his life. He could care less if one of the soldiers were more physically fit than himself. All he cared for was the pursuit of life's pleasures, not its burdens. Although, he was oblivious to the burden he placed on others."

"I'm sorry, I'm not following you," I admitted. Petey wasn't making much sense, due in part to his jubilant demeanor while delivering such a morbid tale.

"What I'm saying is, the dictator was even larger than you, but had no self-conscience perceptions of himself when in the presence of those more, well, muscled than himself. He didn't need muscles. He had what he coveted and wasn't going to relinquish it for anyone but himself. In short, don't think you need to conform yourself simply because another has something seemingly glamorous. What you have is yours, and unless you want what you have to be different, do not change."

"So...you want me to stay...fat?" I believe he was getting to that point.

"No," he shook his head, "I want you to decide if you want that. Not for someone else to come along and say, "You should've been that way the whole time", but for you to say "I'm glad *I* made this choice"."

His emphasis on the word "I" made it clear this time around. And my answer: I was staying the course I determined just yesterday. I would eat more vegetables just as long as Steve Jobs and his family were still around. Not longer, and not shorter.

I wasn't sure who this man was, or why he'd come to talk to me when the other kids in the group were more willing to speak with him. He was a different kind of adult. Nicer. Kinder. Not like Mrs. Jobs, though. His kindness, it seemed to come out with more...something... in his voice. I couldn't pinpoint what it was. I would later. I would know what was different about the voice when it came my time to deliver it to another. It came out for one of the jungle children. His name was Dende.

CHAPTER 4
Backs of photos

There were about four or five more days before Steve and his parents left our little community so Steve could reach bigger and better scholarly heights. And as sad as I was about it, it was good for him. I'd be happy to tag along with him to the Cupertino academy, but my grades were nowhere close to his. I tried my best to get a 4.0 this past semester, but after failing that quiz of Mr. James's, I couldn't recover in time enough to raise my grade up high again.

I had continued to do as Mrs. Jobs said and replaced more and more food items with vegetables and fruits. I was up to two vegetables: carrots and lettuce, and three fruits: apples, oranges, and cherries. I especially loved cherries. Cherry poptarts, cherry pie, and cherry danishes. But the cherries I was referring to were the ones that grew straight off of the tree. I'd always made my mom inspect the cherries from the grocery store to ensure that they were indeed fresh. If I was going to forego one of more of my sweets, I had to make sure it was only for the best produce that I could get my hands on.

Today was Friday, but Steve called yesterday to say he would be busy packing so we could have the weekend to hang out together. His parents said that since this was our last weekend together for a while, that they would allow him to sleep over at my house while they packed up even more of their things in the meantime. Friday was pretty much uneventful. Some meals, some cartoons, some gardening with my mother, and then boom, Saturday had come at last.

Once Steve had arrived, some time in the early afternoon, I had to show him something incredible, at least that I thought was incredible. I took him straight to the bathroom and I made him focus on the scale's monitor as I stepped up onto it. My up and down weight had finally dropped to a considerably lower number than before. I was no longer between the 160-185 weight range, I was now as low as 155.

Just like the day at the rink, Steve clapped, but his smile resembled the one I got from Petey some months ago. I still remembered that smile. The way it invited a joyous sensation to those who witnessed it. The perfect example of an infectious good mood that could spread like an epidemic. Steve's smile no longer appeared like a gas mask meant to repel the infection, but mirrored it flawlessly.

"That's great, Jack," he said.

"You'll have to thank your mom for me. Without her advice, I'd never have started on this path," I replied. And it was true. That one McDonald's pit stop was a stepping stone for me to the path I needed to be on, but that day was an advancement not just for me, but for Steve, too.

"So, what would you like to do today?"

"I don't know," I stated. "What do you do with a friend who's going to be gone in a couple of days?"

"Umm, watch a new movie. Tell stories- Ooh, we could visit the city arcade, or go skating again. I don't know. There's too much to choose between."

And that's Steve's most tragic flaw. His indecisiveness. Although, we seemed to mutually share that instinct currently. I was coming up with other suggestions, all just as mundane. Things like: soccer, watch reruns of our favorite television shows, etc. We were hopeless.

"Oh," Steve said with complete sense of incredulity. "Have I not given you the number of where we'll be living yet?" he asked. I shook my head and then he recited the following numbers. "It's eight-one-eight-one-two-two-nine-three-four-six."

I asked him to repeat it so I could write it down i my address book. I found his name on the first page- he was the only person in it presently- crossed out his old number and wrote eight-one-eight-one-two-two-nine-three-four-six underneath the crossed or portion.

"So, what's Cupertino look like? You said you went up there for a tour last weekend, didn't you?" I was curious. This school had better be amazing if it was splitting the two of us apart.

"It was soooo cool," he stated. "There's a large campus and plenty of boys around my age who also passed the entry exam. My grades were one of the best, so I had the choice to jump from fifth grade to seventh, but I wanted to make peers out of people the same age as me, so I convinced my parents to let me only be promoted to the next grade up only. I could start my term in middle school correctly. As a freshman," he boasted pleasantly.

"Then I'll still be graduating one year before you," I teased. Honestly, I was hoping Steve and I would just go through every level of education together, from elementary, when we met in the third grade, but he was in first, all the way up until our then highly fantasized but now very realistic dream of going to college. I was certain that one or both of us were going to take that leap.

"Hey, with my grades, I could still catch up to you," Steve joked. The way he was now, I kind of wanted to call him Stevey now. He was half himself and half Petey.

"Wanna bet?"

"Remember the last one you made?"

"Yeah, I lost, but I still finished," I countered.

"Then let's do that for this one, too. No matter who wins, we both have to vow to finish."

"Fine...but we haven't actually settled on a bet just yet," I pointed out.

"What should it be then?"

"The first of us to become successful in whatever field we enter into wins. And by successful...umm, it means whichever of us gets televised about our accomplishments or have an expose written about them first wins. And the field can be anything you want," I explained.

"Well, I'll probably do something tech based." He looked down at his wristwatch. The minute and second hands were both stuck at 8:21am, even though it was well into the afternoon. "I took out a few of the gears to help with another project of mine."

"That's cool," I said. "What's the pro-"

"What field are you thinking about?" he asked with a rush of excitement, eager to hear about the prospects I had in mind for my future.

The truth, I had none.

The lie, "I'm thinking about teaching. Instructing. Something like that."

"Oh, you should teach science. You're pretty good at that."

"You think so?"

"Yeah, I mean, you always get the best of your grades there, don't you?"

I scratched my head. I guess that was true, but I never really thought of it like that. Honestly, as much of a pain as it was to learn, science was always my favorite subject. English was a close second. I didn't have to study, just read and say what I liked about certain books. Math was just too extreme with long division and all those stupid algebraic equations and whatnot. History, aside from that field trip, was as boring as watching paint dry.

"I'll think about it."

And I did. All weekend long. It was all Stevey and I could talk about. We talked all the different branches of science there were, more than the three we studied in school. Aside from chemistry, biology, and anatomy, there was also astronomy, zoology, botany, etc. I considered those six the main ones, as we dubbed them the six simple sciences. All the others were merely branches that could basically be called one of those in the grand scheme of things. Technically, zoology and botany were branches of biology, but the "study of living things" seemed very broad, so we decided splitting it into plants and animals was only fair. More technical terms of sciences geared toward organisms, like reptiles or insects, those didn't need to be part of the main six.

Apart from science and all that it entailed, we finally moved on to some actual games. We played Super Mario Bros., read some of the comics that Stevey was going to pack up the second he got home, and of course, we went skating. Harrison was there, but we were more careful about avoiding another confrontation with him.

We paused from skating for a half hour and bought some snacks from the rink vendor. My mom lent us enough cash to buy half the vendor out of his stock, and I nearly wanted to, but after showing Stevey my new weight loss, I couldn't go and reverse it all now. Not on one of my last days seeing him. Stevey ate nachos and drank some water. I also had a water, but I bought an ice cream cone instead. It was summer and hot, and I was not looking to intensify the degrees that currently made my mouth as dry as snails left out in the sun for far too long.

Stevey graciously threw away our garbage and then joined me at the bench.

"You up for more skating or should we wait a little longer?" he asked.

"Just five more minutes," I told him. Five minutes later, I said the same thing, and five minutes after that. Finally, he said,

"We don't have to skate anymore today."

"Good, because my legs feel like they could buckle under any second now."

"So, what are you gonna do after we leave?" Stevey tried to exude the same enthusiasm he had earlier, but now he was sounding more like regular old Steve Jobs. Which I found nice. I wanted to talk with the friend I grew to respect these past few years. Not that weird Stevey act that he did astonishingly well at.

But, his question was a good one. I had no clue what my weekends would be like when he left. I didn't have any other friends, and sure I didn't want any anyway. However, being lonely was certainly going to be something I'd have to struggle to get used to. Maybe I could try to meet someone else to pal around with. No one from school, that was for sure. Maybe I could try expanding my horizons and meet people in places where I don't know anyone. High school wasn't too far off. Maybe I could make some there.

"Nothing," I finally said.

And that's what I remember of the rest that weekend. If my life were a film, this would be a section of the reel that was suddenly misplaced during editing and forgotten, forever lost. If the film were played during a private screening for the director, they'd suddenly come across a long section of utter blackness. Nothing would be on screen and a waste of his time and resources.

The next thing I recalled was that Tuesday. Steve had left the day before. I sat in my bed, staring out the window. I didn't look down at the backyard or up at the sky, but straight ahead, out at the skyline of Downtown Los Angeles, which could barely be perceived through the morning haze.

If this were also part of the film, this would be the long, transitional montage scene.

I sat there in my bed, watching the seasons and weather change through my window. Whether it rained, stormed, or was clear, the haze would not leave. Downtown Los Angeles was perpetually shrouded by the sheet of fog, like it was wrapped in a bubble where the condensation was neverending.

In my bathroom, the number the scale read was still 155. It stayed that way until about a week and a half later, when it had dropped to 153. I called Steve and informed him of my progress and he would do the same to me. He'd told me all about their new home, how it was every bit as good as their last one, from the marble steps to the bridge-style walkway on their second floor. Their kitchen and living room tables were topped by mahogany wood waxed so deep that their reflections could be seen even through the dust.

Another week and a half later, I'd dropped another pound or two and tried to call Steve, but his mother said he was unavailable. I figured it was fine. I'd try again in two weeks, but at the time I was supposed to call, I was busy. My mother developed a fever and was hospitalized, so I stayed with her most days. It took nearly a month for her to be released from the hospital, so no matter how hard she'd try to lie, I knew she was burdened by no mere fever. She urged me to put it out of my mind, and so I did.

Not sure how long that took, but once I was back on my way to losing weight and reporting to Steve, the school year had begun. Steve said that he needed time to adjust to his new school and that he'd be busy for a while, so we didn't talk much from September to November. In that same stretch of time, I'd forgone my weight cares, still worried about my mother. Her health was not worsening, but it wasn't improving either. The medication prescribed to her was a stalling method, at best. I tried to once read the label on the pill bottle, but the pronunciation was alien to me. I'd try again when I'd researched it some more.

It was the second semester of seventh grade and January was blazing hot. I'd devoured pounds of ice cream to try and alleviate some of the stress it was causing my body. Throughout the month, I'd avoided the scale as long as I could. It was shortly after February began that I caved. I had to know. I had to talk to Steve. 179, the display read.

I needed to stop. But I couldn't.

I sometimes waited until my bowl of ice cream melted and then slurped up what remained in a matter of minutes. I'd began timing myself to see how quickly I could clear the bowl of even the tiniest trace of the milky delight.

It was around April when I finally got up the courage to call Steve again. I'd gained even more pounds, closer to 210 by that point, I believe. I kept that to myself as we talked. He told me that he'd met some kid named Wozneyak, or something like that. I didn't care about his new friend. I was his friend and that's all that mattered to me. He said that the Wozniak guy- he told me how to spell it the second time he brought him up- was into technology just like him and that they were working on some projects together now. I nearly slammed the phone on the hook.

Steve Jobs never let me in on his technological projects. I mean, he would show them to me from time to time, but he never once allowed me to help out. I know that I didn't have much of a clue about how most technologies operated, but he could've taught me.

After about a half hour of listening to him brag on and on about the Wozniak kid, he said that he had to go have dinner with his father. I simply obliged, not feeling so well with what he'd just told me. If anything, this told me exactly how the bet was going to pan out. I was going to lose. Steve was already making friends to help further his skills, but here I was, over seven months later, and not even closer to deciding which science fascinated me most, or if they still did at all.

Since the latter half of seventh grade commenced, I'd lost the extreme interest in science I once held. I was still peculiarly fixated on the simple machines, but that was about it. I'd even lost interest in researching whatever was ailing my mother. She finally seemed to be getting healthier, so I guessed that was why. As for the other school subjects, none of them got any better, but at least English didn't get any worse. I'd begun considering teaching English recently. I'd tell Steve the next time I spoke with him.

That time never came.

In the summer months following seventh grade, I tried twice a month to call him, but neither time had anyone answered, not even to produce or proffer some lame excuse. They left me hanging entirely. I went into my eighth grade school year without a single friend, in school or out, but I wasn't depressed.

I'd suffered an eternity of fat jokes, mean and degrading names, and teachers with foul attitudes. The things tossed at me in eighth grade were simply pebbles washing onto a shore with thick sand. They may have reached me, but they got stuck in the earliest trenches I had, not even coming close to hitting the mark the bigots desired. The year was a breeze.

At my middle school graduation, which took place in a three star hotel auditorium, my photos were all about me. All they were was of me, filled to the frame tightly by my figure, a young man with medium-length girth, a package of tightly packed meat, weighing in at close to 243 lbs. I wasn't happy, I wasn't ashamed. I was me. I was smiling.

The photos to come over my next four years at high school were all the same. I was the only person in each one. Not to say I was totally lonely. I made a few "friends", but nothing that would transcend beyond our high school graduation. I mapped my progress each year with an end-of-the-year photo. On the backs of them, where people would usually scribble down who took the photo or when and where it was taken, I scribbled down how much I weighed on the backs. Ninth grade- 255. Tenth grade- 270. Eleventh grade- 266 (I dropped only because I didn't want to take gym my senior year, so I got it out of the way). Twelfth grade- 281.

The class of 83' held a mock election and you can guess what I got: class whale. It was accurate, at least. Only whales could put on this much girth and weight in that time span. Well, they could've gone with elephants, or rhinos, or hippos, but I guess those three animals were all to fearsome to describe me. A creature attacking a hippo thinking that its weight gave it a disadvantage was in for a rude awakening. A whale was so huge, that any jabs at its body would be nearly imperceptible, unless attacked by a great pain.

My great pain came my freshman year of college. I did keep my promise to Steve, even though we were no longer in contact. I got into the Los Angeles City College. I wasn't staying in a dorm room. I had a job in a local coffee shop and worked there on weekends to pay for my one room apartment. I wasn't a server, but a cook. I wasn't huge for no reason. My mother had taught me to cook on weekends throughout high school, and I was good enough for a coffee joint. I was actually just getting off work one Saturday afternoon when I got the call that broke me.

The funeral was small, mainly me, my grandparents, some relatives- cousins or whatever- and the pastor they had found to officiate the ceremony. We buried her promptly. Although it was blazing outside, I stood there for about two hours after my relatives uttered some condolences and wandered back off to their own lives.

At the next funeral I would attend, for one of the jungle children, I would do the same thing. Come. Honor. Grieve. Turn away.

My mother was the last and only person I could have conversations with. I made no friends at work, classes, or anywhere. I certainly wasn't about to reach out to the relatives that were practically strangers before today. I needed to be alone. Now. Tomorrow. Next week. Forever.

I knew I couldn't handle the onslaught of college while suffering the pain of losing a mother. I dropped out within the week, quit my job, went back home, and balled myself on my old bed, which she kept in the same condition as it was in when I left for college. The same blank walls, the same bed sheets patterned with bubbles in assorted colors, and my same tv that rested on the nightstand beside my closet.

I stepped out and headed down the hallway, straight for her room. I grabbed the handle and pushed the door slightly ajar. I raised my left foot to step inside, but it froze in place, in mid air. I couldn't lower or advance it. I was catatonic, mortified, terrified to look inside.

The hospital said that she died of, um, what did they call it? Some sort of pulmonary something-or-other. Embolism, maybe? Yeah, that was it. As you can tell, I was still unknowledgable about medical terms. She suddenly couldn't breathe halfway through the stroke she was suffering. She managed to give the 911 operator her name and address before losing the ability to communicate. She was rushed to the hospital, but once there, the damage was too far beyond reparation. The doctors tried to ease her passing as best they could, they assured me. I mean, they didn't say that exactly. It was something like "We made sure that she was as comfortable as could be." Then they apologized and left me there to grieve in peace.

I finally lowered my foot and shut the door on myself. I'd go in, but not today. Perhaps tomorrow. Or next week. But it soon became never. I was unable of mustering up the courage to peer into her dwelling any more than I could pick up the phone and dial up Steve, hoping an old familiar voice would console me. It may have, but I wasn't strong enough to seek comfort. Besides, I had one issue to tackle that I was more than proud to do, put my mother's home back on the market.

It took weeks to sort out the mess that was my mother's life insurance policy, along with trying to clear out the place as best I could without entering her room. I had asked some former co-workers if they could help in exchange for $150 apiece. They both agreed to do it for half that given the situation. I packed my room the quickest, but it was pretty scarce pickings. The only thing that mattered to me was the tv. I didn't have one in my apartment to limit the distractions to my studies, but I was hardly going to need that now.

We all quickly packed up the pieces of furniture I could make use of in my one room flat. The rest was put up for sale the next day. I made close to $4,000 dollars off of all the curtains and crap that my mother loved. I didn't want any extra reminders of her in my life from this point onward. Her bed sheets, her bed, her clothing, and all the other things she seemed to treasure, it was all sold.

I paid my helpers and then took up residence inside the house for a few hours. I was bone ass tired and my legs and arms ached horrendously. I was not going to enjoy my drive home one bit, no matter how much rest I allowed myself to take. Instead, I ignored the pain and took one last walk around the house. Since we'd emptied it pretty thoroughly, there wasn't much but wallpaper and reasons to vacuum to see.

I finally made my way to the backyard, having forgot it was there in the chaos of the yard sale. I wandered over and expected my mother's plants. Many of them were wilted, bent over forward as if they too mourned her passing. A few others still stood erect, but I imagined how long it would take before they began missing their mother's care, as well. I smiled at the absurdity. These flowers were able to keep themselves together far longer than I could hope for if I had the emotional strength of one thousand versions of myself. It only took one huge strike to cripple so badly that I could barely function.

The entire day after receiving the news, I could not have been in worse shape. I hung up on the doctors relaying the events to me. I knew they'd tell me later, but I still couldn't believe the words I heard when I answered.

"Is this Jack Garbarino?" the doctor asked. Based off the voice, they were female.

"Speaking," I said with the confidence that, in a moment, was going to jump off of a twenty-story building to its demise.

"I'm sorry to inform you, but at 10:16 am this morning, your mother, Mrs. Elaine Garbarino, passed away."

I'd tried to neglect it, but the fact was, I had to go to the hospital. It wasn't until the day after they informed me via phone that I made myself stand before her body, down in the morgue, placed in the lower levels of the building. It was another movie scene. I felt that at any moment, she was going to rise again. That she wasn't truly dead. That this was some weird prank she decided to pull on me. It actually was in character for her. Her pranks often made no sense to me. When Steve left, she thought that it was his prankster side to him I missed most, so she tried to compensate.

She would do things like pretend that mouse traps had snapped shut over her fingers, that she burned her elbow on the iron, or that she slipped and fell down the stairs. She pulled that one so often that I once took it for a prank when it actually happened. She didn't break anything, but her shoulders were worse for wear for a few days.

I had arrived at the insurance office to collect the funds the moment they were ready. I needed the money to pay rent and survive, while also trying to sort out what I needed to next do with my life. I wasn't going to find anything by pointlessly doing readings for classes or studying for tests. The best any of those tasks could tell me was how well I processed and retained information. I needed something to grant me purpose, something to say that I was maybe doing something worthwhile. Thanks to the insurance, I now had a good deal of money, more than I needed to survive on. Perhaps others could benefit from it just as much.

And they would. But it'd take some time. I wasn't the man I needed to be for others to follow. I was still a follower myself. I didn't have much in the way of leadership. No confidence to take up that mantle.

But I was on my way. The jungle children were going to need me, if they didn't at this point, but the jungle children certainly needed me when I arrived.

CHAPTER 5
My attention

Life was slow going lately. I couldn't find pleasure from anything. Eating. Sleeping. Television. Masturbating. Nothing. Hell, my days were so predictable that I could recite the ingredients in most tv dinners off of memory alone. For example, a Tony's microwavable pizza's ingredients are as follows: tomatoes, enriched flour, imitation mozzarella, fat reduced pepperoni, shortening, yeast, sugar, modified food starch, vegetable oil, salt, spice, maltodextrin, hydrolyzed soy, corn protein, garlic powder, paprika, dough conditioner, and ascorbic acid. There are a lot of parentheses as to what many of those individual ingredients contain, but that's just too technical for me.

It's been about a week since finalizing the insurance money and I had already started using it for mundane means. I'd been ordering plenty of tv dinners in bulk to be delivered from the stores. I was too lazy and too nauseous to even attempt to move from my love-seat couch. It needed to be a love-seat to fit me. I had lost whatever shreds of self control I had in college and put on even more pounds. I didn't know the exact number, but I was north of 300, undoubtedly.

The only times I got up were to warm up more microwavable dishes or to use the restroom. The only times I needed the latter were in the morning, twice during the day, and again at night. I'd hammered that into my body like a drill sergeant hammers discipline into his soldiers. The moment that thought entered my head, I snorted with glee that I wasn't a soldier. That life could suit me any less.

But, in a sense, I guess my body was my soldier and I was forcing it to a certain standard. Maybe today was time for a change of scenery. Staring at a low-tech television and watching the news day in and out gets dull, no matter how "exciting" the story they claim to have.

I broke my bathroom schedule and took a shower. It took time to reach the harder areas on my back. It generally takes me about forty-five minutes to shower, and during that time the hot water tends to die out. The only good news is that by that point, my body has retained enough heat from the scalding rinse that it doesn't bother me. I dried- a ten minute affair- and then got dressed, which is actually pretty quick in comparison.

I grabbed a phone book from beneath my couch. I typically only used it to find the numbers of places that delivered. A week was long enough to stay cooped up in this place. I needed to get out more than I thought. I scanned the pages for addresses that were in my vicinity. I found one, wrote it down on a sticky note, and left.

I sat in a booth in the rear of a restaurant called Casa di Nova. It was fairly empty, so there was no one around to poke fun at me not-so-subtly. The restaurant was decorated with an assortment of crimson and beige furniture. Half of the booths had beige leather seats, and the other half crimson. The drapes at the windows were all silk and crimson with beige cords tying them to the walls, so the window view of the street was wide open. On the walls between the windows and near the restroom area were old Greek paintings and sculptures. I recognized one of them from one of my recently dropped college courses. It was of a man extending his hand out to touch the fingertips of another. I don't remember who the painter was or when it was made, but it was iconic enough for me to remember.

I took time deciding what I wanted to order. It was tough. They had so many pizza options, from Mexican to Italian to a veggie and meat lovers version. The waitress came over, a yellow pad in her hands.

"What would you like to drink?" she asked gingerly, as if nervous to be around me.

"Is your water free?" I asked in return. I'd been willing to spend cash on bulk packages of tv dinners, but spending a couple of dollars on water was suddenly wrong. Yeah, I had issues.

"Yes, sir. It is. Would you like a glass?"

I nodded.

She left and returned with a glass of water, but swimming in the liquid was a lemon. The most accursed fruit that ever did exist. I once tried one and the impact of the sour flavor was so intense that my first experience with Indian food left my eyes watering less. I held up a hand and pointed at the lemon.

"Could you remove that, please?" I asked with as much masked hysteria as I could muster forth. Lemons were dangerous things.

"Sure. I'll be right back." She definitely sounded more alarmed that time around. My mask must not have fooled her the true identity of my feelings toward the oversight. She returned with lemon free water and placed it on the table.

I was suspicious. "Is this the same glass with just the lemon taken out?" I asked.

With an exasperated huff, she grabbed the glass and returned once more to the kitchen. She was likely not to get a tip with an attitude like that.

I accepted my new glas of water and sipped it as she stood, awaiting my approval. It lacked any trace of that citrus-y aftertaste, so I deemed the drink satisfactory.

"What would you like to eat, sir," she said, and I could sense the stress she faced as she forced out the word sir.

"I'm gonna need a minute or two," I said curtly. Their menu had too many options. Plus, I hadn't been in a real restaurant for some time, and I needed to ease myself back into it.

As I was deciding on my dish for the evening, a family had entered the restaurant. There were two women and a young girl, I'm guessing the daughter of one of the women, and maybe a niece or aunt. They sat and the waitress went to them and was as pleasant as could be.

"Hi, I'm Devon. I'll be your waitress this evening," she introduced herself politely. I didn't even get to learn her name until just now. She took down their drink orders, brought them to them, and then wrote down what pizza they desired. I think the settled on Mexican. Since I didn't wish to be a copycat, I'd order Italian. I told that to Devon when she finally came by and asked for my order once again.

I sat there waiting a good ten or so minutes for my food. Half the time was spent making use of their open curtains to watch the cars whiz by. I saw a few fancy ones, sports cars like Corvettes. I didn't usually pay attention to details of vehicles, but I knew that Corvettes always came with rounded headlights, and that was about the only indication I found to identify them with.

The other half of the time went to listening in on the conversation the two women and the child were having. I was in and out of focus there, so I only heard broken pieces of dialogue.

"What's Africa?" I heard the child ask, as innocent as could be.

"It's a continent, sweetie," said one of the older women. Her one feature I found to stand out was her pink leather jacket.

I zoned out briefly, and when I came back, the other woman had said "Those poor jungle children."

I didn't want to continue listening. It seemed like it was a disheartening topic, and I had finally forced myself to leave my apartment. I was in no rush to go back there.

Devon approached with a large platter on her right hand. That alone astounded me. I was left handed mainly, but whenever I tried using my right hand, I could never do anything close to that impressive. he set down the pizza on the table before me and it looked amazing.

It was baked with tomatoes on top of the cheese, and the tomatoes were accompanied by fresh basil and garlic, not to mention a couple of bell peppers scattered around the pie. I was ready the moment I saw the perfectly golden brown crust. That part alone was worth the $12.95 I paid.

But still, I had to ask "Would you recommend this to other customers?"

Devon clicked her tongue before she said "I'd recommend this to someone a quarter of your size, but not to anyone half or more your size in direct proportion." She huffed and turned away.

I ignored her sharp words, but they certainly reached higher up the shoreline than most insults recently. I looked up slightly and could hear the hushed laughter coming from the women's table. I put them and Devon out of my mind.

I took no time eating through the pizza. I was tired of staying out in public for today and just coveted the warm embrace of my loveseat couch back home. Nothing was going to be more pleasing than that right now. I quickly paid my bill, but I waited long enough to make Devon angry enough to come to me to get it. She scowled at the discovery that there was no tip coming, but she deserved that herself.

I went back home. I sat down. I counted to ten. I reflected on today. I hadn't once considered it before, but what if I deserved that treatment even more than Devon. I mean, she was only doing her job- at first, anyway- and I did kind of act annoyingly. I was a grown man trying to live my life and suddenly, I was just nothing but this poor man living off my mother's life (insurance). I needed to further my life somehow. Maybe I could get my job back at the coffee joint.

The next morning, I gave them a ring and asked for Remmy. He was busy at the moment, but he gave me a call back an hour or so later.

"Jack?" he asked, sounding surprised. "How are you?"

"Oh, I'm doing fine," I said. "How's it going with you?"

"Not bad, not bad."

"Hey, Remmy, I was wondering if I could get my job back," I said to bring the call to the point before we got lost in trivial niceties.

"I would love to man, but we filled your position about a week later. No openings right now," Remmy stated.

My heart sank, and so did my voice.

"Jack. Jack, you there?" Remmy asked. He repeated the question a few more times before I heard the click of his hanging up.

That was practically the only job I could get as a mere high school grad, much less now that I was a college dropout. I could try fast food, but that seemed a joke even to me. I didn't need a job around food anymore. Part of what pushed beyond the 300 lb mark was that at the coffee house I got to get free lunch there. If I were to be awarded those same benefits elsewhere, there was no limit to what weight I could achieve.

I turned my thoughts to things within my control now. I still had a good amount of money. I could perhaps return to college. I could live off of it until I found a job. Or, I could simply give it all away and force myself into desperation. One of the few things I remembered about biology class was that when an animal- and humans are technically animals- are backed into a corner, they tend to fight for survival. But how could I give it all away?

That's when the phone rang. It was the woman I dealt with from the insurance company. Her name was Amber Gregginson.

"Hi, may I speak with Jack Garbarino, please?" she asked. Her voice was soft, but the way she spoke made her request seem like a command.

"Speaking," I replied.

"Hi, Jack, or do you prefer Mr. Garbarino?"

I told her Jack the first time we met. I told her again. "Jack is fine, Mrs. Gregginson."

"Actually, I'm back to being Ms. Amber Gregginson now. My divorce was finalized two days ago," she stated. I was amazed by how casually she made her marital failure seem.

"Well, what can I do for you, *Ms.* Gregginson," I corrected.

"I'm calling on behalf of your mother's former home. Remember that when we last spoke that you had to remove all possessions before we could officially open the home up to tours," she explained. She could remember that, but my name preference was just too small a detail for her intensely detail-oriented eyes.

"Yes, and I did just that. All the possessions were either taken by me or sold the very next day," I said. I was sure I'd cleared out my room, the kitchen, the living room, and her bed…"Oh, I apologize. I thought I had thoroughly gathered up everything in my mother's room."

"It's fine. The only item left behind was a sunset colored jewelry box with the initials E.G. carved into it. I assumed it stood for Elaine Garbarino."

"Yes, that's hers for sure. She kept a lot of her favorite accessories in there." I wiped away tears that I had noticed fell until I tasted salt on my lips. "Um, I can go there and collect it tomorrow."

"That's not necessary. I can come to you. I inspected the home this morning and found it. I had to dig through my records to make sure that it did indeed belong to you and that some squatter didn't leave it behind. What time would you like for me to come and drop it off?"

"Oh," I was surprised by her offer. It didn't seem like her kind of thing to do, to just drop her duties for a side stop. "I'm usually up around 8 am if you're a morning person. If not, anytime after 11 am would work just as well," I said. I wanted her to come early. I didn't want to waste her time like I was doing with mine.

"I'll see you bright and early at 8 am. You still live in your one room apartment, correct?"

I nodded and then realized that I was having a phone conversation. Her voice was so soothing, even through the phone, that it sounded like she was right next to me. "Yes, I do. Looking forward to seeing you."

But not as much as she was, apparently. She came banging on my door a little before 8 am had even come around. I walked over as fast as I could and opened the door.

"Hi, you're early," I said, still half asleep. I'd only barely slept last night. I think whatever was in that Italian pizza did not agree with me. I woke up several times in the night with unbelievable stomach aches. That, along with Devon, meant I was never going there again.

"I figured the earlier the jog, the better," she replied. She was dressed in latex shorts, a pale green tank top that hugged her breasts tightly, with sweat lining the space beneath her cleavage. Her hair was done up in a ponytail, but her bangs clung to her face, affixed to her forehead via the sweat. Underneath her right arm was the jewelry box. She removed it with her left hand and extended it toward me. "Here you go."

I grabbed it with a smile. "You're a leftie, too, huh?" I asked.

She wiped her forehead with her elbow. "Oh, yeah. I'm actually right-handed, but I use my left hand more so I can technically call myself ambidextrous. Helps to impress men," she said and winked. I'd never flirted with a woman before, but I was going to count this conversation as such.

"I'm a pure leftie. I mean, I can use my right hand for a few things, but probably not as well as you use your left." She was right. I was impressed.

"So, I've got about another hour before I need to head to work. Would you like to join me for the rest of my jog? I'll run at your pace so you don't feel bad," she said. She didn't sound mean or insulting, but genuinely sincere, much like Petey had been.

"If we went at my pace, you'd end up being late for work, trust me," I replied. I was not about to test her willpower when it came to holding back hysterical laughter. "Perhaps a time when you're more free." I didn't expect her to make a counter proposal.

"Fine, we'll go jogging Saturday morning, and I'm not letting you say no. So, if you don't have any athletic clothes, go and buy some. I'll see you Saturday." She waved as she sprinted away from my door and down the steps, out of sight.

I shut the door gingerly, crossed to my loveseat, and sank down onto the cushions. I didn't intend to go jogging, but her smile and voice was too tempting. Although, it probably had more to with than just her voice. I shook my head fiercely. How could I say yes? I should've been more assertive with my refusal, but with her quick speech and perky attitude, it was hard to get a word in. I didn't antici-pate things to go so awry this day. I simply wanted to get my mother's jewelry box back.

I lifted the jewelry box and stared at the engravings of her initials. They must've been done by a pro, because the style of the lettering was so precise. It was as if they'd done it with one swift motion, both for the "e" and the "g". I couldn't get it this good with my left hand, much less my right.

I peeled the lid of the box back and inside was a collection of just what I mentioned earlier, my mother's favorite jewelry. Inside were two of the necklaces I made her back when I had attended Sunday school. That was a time back when my father was alive. When he passed, we sort of forgot about the faith, but this made it all come rushing back.

My father, Jeremy Garbarino, was as righteous as one could be. Devoted to the lord, sometimes to a fault. He was a deacon, he was an usher, and even a member of the choir. He was the ultimate as much as church goers went. He would drag my mother and I along with him and I would be forced to attend Sunday school with the other children while he and my mother would confess their sins and wrongdoings before a deity that my mother didn't even believe in. I didn't believe in one either, but my disbelief was simply because my father had perished in a store robbery before I was even 7 years old. What deity would let such a devoted soldier die to something like that? When that happened, I joined my mother on the atheist bandwagon.

I grabbed the necklaces made from plastic beads on a thin wire string and tossed them into the garbage. Both people that they made me remember were gone, and I didn't need emotional episodes for both parents. I'd suffice with just my mother for the time being.

I continued to rummage through the jewelry box for other doomed accessories, but they all passed my inspection, from the bracelets she bought shortly after my tenth birthday. She said that she wanted something to show off at her job. She was a mail carrier, so she would be wearing them while traversing streets, carrying loads of mail in a flimsy little bag. I hadn't once thought about it, but she could've been mugged for those bracelets at any point. Not to speak ill of the dead, but in hindsight, that wasn't the smartest choice.

After that, I found some earrings I hadn't seen her wear in the years before her passing. She always tried to look good on the job, especially after being promoted to post office supervisor. Her jewelry taste jumped up a few calibers, but she always preferred simple designs to over the top ones. Which is why I threw away the next piece I found.

It was a pair of hoop earrings with dragon molds whirling around the hoops. The hoop bands were bronze, but the dragons were a bright emerald. The colors clashed so fiercely with what my mother usually were. I felt about as bad tossing those out as I did the bead necklaces.

Finally content with what I discovered inside, I shut the box and placed it on a bookshelf mounted onto the wall. I placed it at the very top with other things I found to be of great importance. Also on the topmost shelf are my photo albums of my pictures with my weights written on the opposite side, my high school diploma, and a stand alone photo of me and my mother. We were at Universal Studios when it was taken, somewhere near the entrance, I believe.

I turned my back to the top shelf and went into my room. I stayed there most of the day, but when dinner time came, my stomach was all too influential about what I should do. I wanted to step outside again, so I pulled out the phone book, fingered the page listings until I found something I could be pleased by. A Umami Burger, I think it was called.

I sat in the outside dining area where few people were likely to be with the chill this night produced. I was well equipped to deal with it, even without my jacket. Lots of natural protection. I scanned the menu, from the California burger to the steak fries. Incidentally, those were the two things I ordered.

The steak fries were nothing I hadn't experienced before, but the California burger. There were few words I could think up to use as a negative comment on it. The carmelized onions, the sauce they called Umami sauce, the meat itself, it all came together better than any burger I'd ever had in all my life. I looked at the menu and learned why. This establishment had just opened up fairly recently and I could see it becoming a national franchise if someone were simply to be smart enough to invest in it. I would, but I don't think that'd be a wise use of my mother's money. I'm still back and forth between college and a job. The waiter had returned to refill my glass of water.

"Excuse me," I said softly, trying not to spew what was between my teeth into his face. "Are you guys currently hiring?" I'd sacrifice a few pounds if they came from this food.

"I'll go and ask the manager. Just a moment," he replied. This guy was certainly getting a tip. Take a page, Devon.

He returned swiftly, but his smile was gone, and that gave it away. "I'm sorry, sir, but we've filled up on all positions. You can check back in about a month or two if you'd like."

I was upset. "The only thing I'd like is the check."

I was done with job hunting. Tuesday and Wednesday both came up horribly on that front, and I dragged my stunted legs all over, to any place that just may need someone like me on their workforce. Sadly, assistance from a morbidly obese 20 year old was not what anyone sought desperately. And I called the college on Wednesday. Re-enrolling meant have to apply all over again, and I'd have to site which classes I'd already taken, along with other technicalities that bored me. I think one was something about having to start my curriculum over from scratch, so my class credits I previously earned would be worth-less now. That effectively knocked out my two most favorite options amongst the ones I listed. The third favorite was give it away, but I had yet to determine a charity I could really get behind and stick with for years to come. Not to say that I'm for guns, or animal cruelty, but those topics only spur up sudden, short-burst responses from me, like when you see someone crying, you feel bad as you watch them cry, but the moment you turn away, it's no longer even on your radar. I wanted something that would always draw me to it, to always beep on my display board, no matter where it was I went...

Wait, the girls at Casa di Nova did say something about Africa. I could look up charities that strictly support them. I think that one of the many news reports I see, doesn't matter what news channel, is that the jungle children of Africa are starving and in desperate need of help. I know they sometimes list the charities and organizations that tend to their needs, so I'll have to keep my eyes open for that.

Thursday had came and went pretty quick. The only thing of interest I did, besides intently flip from news channel to news channel in case any of them showed what charities I might join with, was when Ms. Gregginson gave me another ring.

"Hello?" I asked.

"Hi, Jack, it's Ms. Gregginson," she said.

"Hi, how are you?" I was pleased she remembered my name this time around.

"I'm doing fine. Um, I'm sorry if this is imposing on your time, but I'm actually in your area and one of my clients just called to cancel a tour of your mother's former home. Would you like to grab lunch?"

"Oh, um, I don't know," I said. I honestly didn't. I hadn't thought of eating until the news had ended, but I did promise to get out more than I did last week. "Sure. Where would you like to go?"

"There's this wonderful little Italian place I've heard good things about. It's called Casa di Nova, and they -"

"Would you like Mexican. I'm feeling more like Mexican," I blurted out. I wanted nothing less than to go back to Casa di Nova. I'm sure that by now, Devon had posted a "banned" sign with my photo underneath. And since they didn't have security cameras, I'm betting she just simply used some sort of crude drawing of a cartoonish fat man.

"Sure. Anything but American," she joked. I laughed. It wasn't a real laugh, but it felt nice to do, feigning amusement or otherwise.

She came and picked me up in her large bus of a van. I sat in the second row of seats because I was not going to fit beside her in the front. Her van was a nice cherry red color and had nice beige seat inside. She was dressed in a dress suit with nearly imperceptible grey pinstripes. The jacket and skirt themselves were brown. Her blouse was a shade between powder blue and pearl. Her hair was shoulder-length and was as curly as my hair was shaggy. I apologized to her for my lackluster appearance.

"It's not a problem," she said. "I've seen much worse on people much uglier than you."

I'd have been more grateful for the comment if she had said "people nowhere near as pretty" than "people far more ugly". If she had said pretty, I would've thought myself pretty. But ugly was the word sticking in my mind right now. Regardless, I said "Thank you."

"So, where's this Mexican place that got you so riled up?" she asked with a playful tone to her voice.

I forgot that my outburst was taken seriously. I needed to think of one quickly. Lucky for me, I knew nearly all the good eateries this community had to offer. I suggested to her that we go and taste test one that I hadn't been to yet. It was called Carne Michoacan.

The atmosphere of this place was definitely fit for a casual lunch outing. Lots of tvs everywhere with sports games on them, a bar with a counter, most like the smoking area. The waiters all had those aprons that came stocked with a certain amount of straws when they started their shifts. We took a two=person table near the kitchen doors.

"Hey, would you like to swap spots with me," I asked Ms. Gregginson. "I'd sit here, but I'm afraid that if they open the door too widely, they'll hit my sides. And that's just uncomfortable for both parties."

She giggled. "Not a problem." We both stood and exchanged places, like the world's most boring round of musical chairs. No losers. No winners. "So, how's your week been thus far?"

"Not too great," I admitted. I was too tired with the disappointments to lie. "I've been trying to decide what to do to try and get my life back on track. No job and no college, so I can't expand my horizons professionally or further my education."

"Why not just focus on yourself then? And by that, I mean you, as in just your person. Like...physically."

And her motives could not have come out more clear for inviting me here to lunch. Another person looking to say how I could eat better to try and decrease my weight. I tried that once. It hadn't worked nearly well enough. I was not likely to give that another go anytime soon, if at all. Still, I couldn't resist her all too enticing voice, so I said "What would you suggest?"

"Well, I think the best way to put off the pounds and put on the muscle is with a gym membership," she stated coolly. "How do you think I keep up this body that you've ogled no less than five times since we got out of the car." She cleared her throat. "Not counting the three times you've done it since we came in here."

I was totally flabbergasted. She'd seen all those...and counted. How was I gonna live that down? And here I thought I was being discrete. But then again, how hard was it to tell that my head had shifted to gaze loving at her...

"Let's chalk that up to four," she blurted out with a playful nature.

I shot my head back up immediately. "I'm sorry. I usually don't, well... I think you can guess what I'm about to say."

"I want you to say it out loud so you can hear how it sounds to say it yourself." Her voice was more motherly this time, like she was slow walking me to some sort of epiphany.

"I'm never been in the company of women as beautiful as you. They see me, and...it's like they're facing the plague, a leprous sickness that they'd best avoid. They're the people who want no notions of their social or private lives ruined by mere association. It's-"

"OK. OK. That's more than enough," she said and laughed a nervous laugh. "Wow, you truly had it rough to compare yourself with leprosy. I'm sorry I made you say that. I just thought you had the normal life of a chubby kid growing up in a harsh generation."

And just like that, the motherly tone was gone, like it was never there. The voice she was using now seemed almost like she was an older sister trying to apologize for being a role model. And in a way, what she made me say was eye opening. There's nothing that can strike home like your own self perceptions. I'd not known all these years that that's how I saw myself. I usually just rolled off insults that came from others and thought that they got caught in the early shoreline. Guess they all piled on top of one another and forced themselves onto my once clear, white sand beaches. I had discovered that they were as muddy as swamps right now. The water soaked insults had permeated my shore so much that fogs rolled along it, as if the sun and sky themselves had cried and the heat from the sand beneath created the mist.

"Um, thank you," I told Ms. Gregg- Amber. I think it was past time that we were on a first name basis.

"No problem. You still wanna eat? We don't have to, if-"

I put up a hand. "It's just a meal. I can survive it." I laughed a true laugh this time and she joined me. "So, Amber, how's your week been thus far?"

And she told me. The house was getting record numbers and very favorable turn outs as she put it. Many of the customers were trying desperately to outbid one another for the property. She said that she'd never once been the estate agent running an auction before and that it was good for her commission. She said that one family, the Laughtons, were most likely to get the property. They only bid every three hours and then outbid the other competitors by nearly twice the amount that was previously posted. She hoped that they would post once more to bring the auction total up to $32,000.

A waiter approached and asked us our drink orders. I asked for a Coke and Amber requested a pink lemonade.

"I used to like pink lemonade," I told her.

"Used to?"

"Pepto bismol was made and pink beverages became taboo for me." She laughed just as the waiter handed her her drink. "Pink lemonade and strawberry milk were loved by me once, but never again." I took my Coke from the waiter and sipped it before laying it down.

"Well, I had once foolishly tried to ingest castor oil and I puked for like four days in a row. Never try that stuff. Taste like vomit your dog let loose on the floor *beside* the toilet."

"Warning noted."

"You know, if you'd like, I could show you a place where you could better your own self image." She slid her drink aside. "It's where I go on weekends. I could take you."

"What's this place called?" I was half curious, half nervous.

"It's a gym called Neptune Fitness. They have several machines that can help with shedding pounds and building muscle."

"I don't know. Gym class was the worst place for me growing up. You wanna know what my nickname was?"

"Sure."

"It was Jack "Porker". Porker was in place of Garbarino."

I looked up at her and suddenly, she wasn't in front of me. Instead, all I saw was Harrison's smug grin. It was the worst thing to see right now. I shook my head and refocused on Amber. I had to put an end to the gym talk right now.

"I'll think about it."

"No," she said. The mother voice was back, but this was the more angry, gonna-teach-you-a-lesson voice. A person I would meet while tending to the jungle children would be able to achieve that same degree of lecturing with just a look.

"No?"

"Jack, I've been trying to be nice about it, but your stubbornness has forced my hand." She scked in a breath and then the waiter walked up to the edge of the table.

"May I take your order?" he asked politely.

I needed to change the subject. "Yes, I'd like-"

"We still need a few minutes." She had shooed him away while holding a stern, motherly leer geared toward me.

"Amber, I don't want to talk about this."

"But you need to. Or, do you intend to ride your mother's insurance to an early grave?"

"Excuse me?"

"I'm not blind, Jack. While your were ogling me at your door, I peered inside your house. I saw the piles of empty tv dinner boxes scattered about like they were magazines you were going to get to again one day, but then you never did. Those aren't good for you. Not in those quantities."

"So what if they're not?" I had no better counter at the moment.

"Look, your mother passed, but do you think she'd be happy to see her son up in heaven again so soon?"

I had her now. "My mother and I are atheists."

"So am I, but if she knew what you were doing, would she really agree with it?"

I flinched at that thought. My mother never once said she was against my weight, but she was always more happy whenever I had actual greens on my plate. It was almost imperceptible, but the way my cheeks puffed when I was angry, my mothers would do something similar when she was pleased. I only caught it a couple of times a week, but she would puff up her cheeks so fast, that if I blinked, it was like it had never really happened. Her face looks the same before and after the split second puff up. Like she'd mastered the technique over years of training. I guess learning to smile like that at church when my father would drag us along was really all the practice she needed.

"It doesn't matter what she'd think," I said coldly. "She's not here anymore. I have to make my own choices."

"So that's it, then. She's dead. She's no longer someone you want to be proud of you. You're going to do nothing to keep her memory alive in you."

"I put her jewelry box, and a picture of me and her, on my "important things shelf" in my apartment."

""Important things shelf"?"

We cut out of the restaurant after we paid for our drinks. I hopped into the second row of seats in her van, her into the driver's seat, and we headed back to my place in silence. Better not to ruin the pace of our, um, argument, until we got there. She parked and I led her to my place on the third floor by way of the elevator. I wasn't so pumped that I'd take the stairs.

I opened my door and led her over to my shelf and gestured for her to check it out. The first thing she looked at was the jewelry box, but she lowered the photograph of my mother and I at Universal Studios. She gazed at it long and hard, for maybe about four, five minutes.

"You were a cute little kid," was her first comment. Her net one was "And you still are." She put the photo back and turned to me.

"I'm not a child anymore," I replied. Her notion that I was a cute kid was ludacris. I was probably younger than Amber, but certainly not by that much.

"I wasn't referring to the kid part," she said, "just the cute part." She ran a hand along my arm and her nails traced ash lines along my skin. "Look, Jack, I'm not judging how you've lived up until now, but right now, maybe you should think of honoring your mother with more than just some shelf space. I mean, aren't there others in your life you would like to keep in your mind, some way, even though you've not seen them for a while."

There was Steve Jobs.

"For me, it would be my grandparents. My parents were both really busy, both the workaholics that thought stocks were more worth their time than bonding with their daughter. My grandparents raised me until they passed in the sophomore year of my high school days. They told me to never let anyone else know a lonely life if I could help it."

"So when you saw my place for the first time?..."

"I knew that I was going to reach out to you, I just didn't know how to do so. Or when."

"Well, I think you chose a good time, but your how is still in question," I declared.

"You can't be serious," she protested. "You're seriously going to continue living like you are now?"

"Why should I change? Because one woman says so?" All right, I knew that was mean, but I was losing my patience.

"No, because you'll die if you continue along this route. I've seen it happen to relatives, and I don't want it to happen to you. How old are you? 20? 21?"

I narrowed my eyes.

"Jack, you can live your life much more fully if you only opened your eyes to the danger your body is in in its current state, but I'm not going to force you. I'll let you learn it on your own."

Amber stepped around me and stopped at my kitchen counter beside the door. I turned and faced her when I didn't hear the sound of the door opening and closing.

"In case you change your mind." She pulled something from her pocket and laid it out on the counter. She nodded and made herself scarce. The moment the door swung shut, I made sure it was closed securely and then inspected the card she left behind. It was a business card for Neptune Fitness. The address, number, and logo branded on it. I tapped it against my hands and hummed.

Friday was a long day. I'd decided that there was something to Amber's speech yesterday. I figured that it wouldn't turn out so well, but I picked up the phone book and searched through for any Steve Jobs. I sound about six or seven. I dialed the first five of them, but they all had disconnected numbers. I dialed the sixth one and only got dead air. The last one was also disconnected. I waited an hour between trying each one, so I wasted around seven hours of my day hoping to contact someone who had abandoned me. I didn't move away from him and then refuse to answer any of his calls. Come to think of it, he never once called me. It was always me calling him.

I had no clue what I was to do about anything regarding him at the moment. It was strange to think that we were so close at one point, and now, would he even remember me if I had reached him? It was a sad thing that that was even a question. I doubt he even remembered the bet we'd made the weekend before he went off to meet that Woz-niak guy. The promise was that no matter which of us became success-ful first, that the other would strive to meet them in stardom, either through a televised press conference or to be written about in some reputable magazine. I wish we had included radio in that list, but who knows where radio will be by the time either of us becomes famous.

He was more than likely bounds ahead of me, because he was prob-ably still in college, still earning 4.0s like they were dollar bill tips for his paper route. You know what, he can be ahead of me for all I care. I had a life. I was living it. Not him. Not my mother. Not Amber. Me. And I was alive, so what shows that she knows nothing but how to blow hot air.

What happened next needed to happen. I was asking for it with all the karmic ranting I was dishing out against other people. Late Friday night, as I was having a cheeseburger I warmed up in the microwave, I felt a weird, cold pain in my legs. Not a hot pain, a cold one. It was my impression that most types of pain, no matter how diverse, came accompanied by a sense of heat. Well, regardless, my legs suddenly felt frozen. I buckled at their chilling numbness and crashed into the floor. I couldn't move.

I needed a phone, but the nearest one was atop the little lamp stand beside my loveseat sofa. Somehow I had to get from here to there. It was about four feet or so between me and my objective. I started to do the only thing I could- roll. I turned my arms inward, the only parts of my body I could move, and used them to propel my body toward the lamp stand. I knocked my girth against it and the phone tipped over. I rose and the next thing I knew, I was dialing 911, but each time I pressed a button, my fingers stung against the plastic keys.

"9-1-1, what is your emergency?" the operator said.

"I..." my throat seemed so tight. "My name's... Jack Garbarino. I c-c-an't move. S-send... help, please." After that, my throat was so tight that any breath that managed to squeeze through was to exit my body, not to enter it. I was suffocating. I don't know what happened between now and the time I awoke in the hospital, but I was in a sort of hun-gover state.

I touched my throat and felt something rubbery against my finger-tips. My sensation of touch was back to normal, but my throat was obviously off. I peered down at my neck and I only saw the ends of what appeared to be a bandage. Was my throat sliced open?

"Yes, it was," a familiar, female voice said.

I turned to my left and there she was, dressed as professionally as she was yesterday.

"Hi, Amber," I said, my voice one pitch away from guttural.

"Did you know you sometimes speak out loud without thinking?" she asked, but I could tell there was a point coming right after she sat down beside my hospital bed. "While you were asleep, you mentioned carrot sticks. No clue why. But then, you brought up the name Stevey, and then you went back to carrot sticks being good… and evil. Then you were pretty much silent."

"How'd you know I was here?" I asked. I didn't want to speak about Steve Jobs, or his Stevey counterpart.

"I was on my way to your apartment when I saw the paramedics wheel out a larger than usual gurney. I put two and two together and followed the paramedics here."

"Why were you headed to my apartment?"

"Because our talk wasn't over. I wasn't going to quit trying to get you to understand your health was in jeopardy, but I guess you know that now. Painfully well, too."

At that moment, one of the doctors walked in. In his lab coat and glasses, he reminded me an awful lot of Mr. James. He had a chart in his hands and stopped at my right. "How are you, Mr. Garbarino? Are you feeling any better?"

"Well enough to leave this place," I said irritably.

"I'm afraid not, Mr. Garbarino. You suffered a complex stroke that nearly left your esophagus out of order. In other words, you were going to suffocate to death if you hadn't gotten to the phone as soon as you did. So, congratulations. You saved your own life."

"How long will I have to stay here, doctor… um…?"

"You can call me Dr. Celso," he said. "And once we can make sure that incision on your neck has healed and is cleaned properly, you'll be good to go. So perhaps around a week or so. But, I must caution you, Mr. Garbarino. The cause of the stroke was partly due because of your obesity. However, the most contributing factors were due to your malnourishment, so I'm having our resident nutritionist draw you up a three-staple diet. You'll need plenty of protein, iron, and calcium over the next couple of weeks." He turned to Amber. "I'm assuming that you'll be making sure he follows the diet to the letter. Right, ma'am?"

"Yes, Dr. Celso," she said.

"Good. Well, that's all the news I have for now. Rest up, Mr. Garbarino. I'll be back in an hour with that list." Dr. Celso gave me and Amber both a courtesy nod before taking his leave.

"I told you so," Amber said, her playful tone was back. But, I suspect would soon be replaced by the mother or the older sister voice. If I had to qualify the playful one as a family member, I would say she'd be the rambunctious younger sister, maybe cousin.

"Yeah, and so what?"

"I'm not going to say it all over again, so here's the summary," Amber said as she leaned in closer. "You're going to die unless you follow the doctor's diet and start working out. Simple as that. Now, I'm walking out that door.   I'll either see you next Saturday at the gym, 2 pm sharp. Or, I'll wish you good luck with your problems and hope you live long enough to meet another pretty woman." And just like she said, she was gone.

I put her out of my mind. It wasn't hard as the moment she stepped through the door, I suddenly became aware of the putrid taste left in my mouth. It wasn't because of my displeasure with her, but it came from something that was fed to me in my unconsciousness. It was worst than that pink spray that dentists spray on your teeth and tongue to clean them. I spent all of an hour trying to forget the taste. That's when Dr. Celso had returned.

"Oh, is your caretaker gone?" he asked, stunned.

"She's not my caretaker, doc," I said. She was the farthest thing from it.

"Oh, um, well, here's the diet I promised. Follow it exactly every day. I'm not saying that if you miss a few minor details, you'll be back here, but just try your hardest to stick to it. OK?" He handed me the list and then went over it with me. He had a second copy on his clipboard, apparently.

"What is Monday's dietary plan?" he asked, fully expecting me to comply. I didn't answer to see what he would do. He gave me a stern look, a very intimidating look, like he was forbidding me from doing that again, even without a word passing through his lips. I suddenly got the impression that his patients did exactly as he ordered as long as he was in the room with him. He repeated himself. "What is Monday's dietary plan?"

I took a breath and then answered. "Breakfast will consist of two egg whites, half of an orange, a glass of soy milk, and toasted wheat bread. Lunch will consist of a banana, one BLT, and soy milk. Dinner will consist of steamed carrots, baked chicken, and either water of soy milk (soy milk preferred)." I gasped when I finished.

"Doc, I've never even tried half the things on this list. How am I supposed to eat things if I don't know I'll like them?"

"Because they will be good for you in the long run," he said. His eyes, however, said that I should just suck it up and do this, or I'll end up back here, but only be a resident of a basement shelf than a hospital bed.

"And why is soy milk the only beverage I can have? What about Coke? Or Dr. Pepper? Or Shasta?"

"Because, those drinks do nothing for your health, Mr. Garbarino," he said. "If you wish, you may drink any fruit juice or water for dinner instead of soy milk, but for breakfast and lunch, it must be obeyed. Do you understand?"

I know he was only trying to inform me, but he came off sounding scarier than even he intended to. I nodded.

"Good. I'd allow orange juice or apple juice, in that case." He lowered and sat down in the chair beside me. "Now, would you read Tuesday's diet, please?"

I sighed. "Breakfast will consist of Breakfast will consist of two egg whites, half of an orange, a glass of soy milk, and toasted wheat bread. Lunch will consist of a banana, one BLT, and soy milk. Dinner will consist of steamed carrots, baked chicken, and either water of soy milk (soy milk preferred)." I blinked.

"Wait, this is the same thing as Monday's menu," I stated. "Why can't I have something else to eat for lunch?"

Dr. Celso laid his clipboard against his chest and gave me an honest look, one that said the verbal sugar-coding was done and over with. "The reason, Mr. Garbarino, is because consistency with this diet is the only way to reverse what you've done to yourself. You consistently

ate nothing but tv dinners in these recent weeks, and probably since
before then, too."

"How'd you-"

"The woman, Ms. Gregginson, gave us some finite amounts of
your life so we could ascertain the cause of your trip to or emergency
room," he elucidated.

"Ah." Of course she did.

"You need a consistent, steady diet to counteract the effects of all
those deplorable fatty acids running amuck in your circulatory system.
Calcium will help strengthen your bones to be better able to support
your weight, even as you shed it. The protein and iron are necessities
for you to be able to allow more oxygen to spread more greatly and
vastly throughout your muscles. It'll make it easier for you to climb a
flight of stairs without being winded before you reach the top."

"And I'm supposed to remember everything that you just explained
to me?"

"Yes, and that's why we're gonna go over every day of the week from
now until you're discharged next week. Now, what is Wednesday's
menu, please?"

And we drilled and drilled and drilled until he had me reciting
the dietary plan from memory. It was a harsh training, but the doc
was unrelenting. Every time he would say how to improve on it, give
me tips. We'd finally managed out a compromise about apple juice or
orange juice. Orange juice was for Monday, Wednesday, and Friday.
Apple juice was for Tuesday, Thursday, and Saturday. Sunday was
meant to all be just soy milk, and I lied and said I could live with that.
Sunday's were now again a day I would dread.

It came time for them to release me back into my natural habitat,
and I was proud to be a wild animal once again. Well, I was anything
but wild, unless you truly did consider me a whale.

I got home after shopping for a week's worth of the ingredients that
I needed to comply with the diet Dr. Celso had hammered into me.
He said that he'd check in about once a week to make sure that I'd been
following the diet. I had no doubt that he'd be able to tell when I was
lying, so I knew better than to try. I cleaned out my fridge of everything I knew would make keeping up this diet impossible. All of my
turkey bacon, burger meat, cheeses, tomatoes, tv dinners, all the other

bad foods that go bump in the fridge.

I took care to make sure I packaged all my new foods into the fridge, layered by shelves. I went and grabbed a marker, some scissors, tape, and a sheet of cardboard. I wrote Monday-Saturday down the cardboard in a vertical line up. I used the scissors to cut between each day and then taped them each to a shelf to be able to better maintain how each day's quantities were used up. I knew that if one day was running low, that I'd need to make another trip to the supermarket.

And done. Half of my commitment was now ready to be held up. I now just needed to begin the other half, my gym membership. It was afternoon on Saturday and I didn't wish to enter that hellish place by myself. I fumbled through my pockets and found the card for Neptune Fitness. I knew the address and it wouldn't take long to get there. I grabbed my phone, pocketed the card, and then said "Hello" once the ringing stopped.

"Jack?" asked a genuinely shocked Amber.

CHAPTER 6

Basic, super, or premium

There we both stood, in the midst of this wide, one story building. The front had the Neptune Fitness sign shining dimly in the afternoon light. Honestly, I felt unbelievably hungry just standing here. That lunch was very unfilling. It was like an appetizer from the usual four course meal (appetizer, salad, main course, dessert) I would eat at any one restaurant.

There were a greater number of individuals spending their Saturday inside this drab, musky building instead of simply resting in their homes or in the park. I wasn't much for parks, myself, but it still seemed better than this.

"So, shall we begin the tour?" Amber asked me.

I was already here, so I had to say "Sure."

She led me from the entrance and we crossed the point of no return. The first group of machines we stopped at were called treadmills.

"These are machines with a track that continually runs underneath your feet, so you have to continually run along it, or it'll toss you onto the floor. They work your legs and chest and back. We'll start with these after the tour," she said.

Next, she took me to an area that was designated "free weights" by a folded out sign at the edge of the area. Beyond were racks of weights, dumbbells, and when Amber escorted me toward them, I could see varying numbers from 10 to 85 engraved in the bulking ends of them. I'm guessing that's how much they all weighed individually. Good luck getting me to grab anything over 15, if that much.

"With these, you can do curls and squat thrusts," Amber stated. "Watch me." She grabbed two of the 15-lb dumbbells and held them at her sides. She would take raise them to be perpendicular to her waist, over her head, down to just over her shoulders and then did the first step again, but she lowered the dumbbells to get them there that time. "See?"

"It looks painful," I said honestly.

She answered honestly. "It is, but rewarding. I don't need to be rushed off to hospitals." She replaced her dumbbells with lighter ones and handed them to me. "Would you like to try?"

I accepted them and raised my arms perpendicular to my waste, and the pain was more than bearable, it was nonexistent. I raised them above my head and there came a twinge of heat within my forearms, but only a twinge. I lowered my hands to over my shoulders and the twinge turned into a kindling ember. My shoulders boomed with it, along with my forearms. It wasn't painful, but it made continuing this a burden. I finished it by lowering them to my waist once more and then forced her to take the dumbbells back from me. I was not going to do that again right away. Once left my shoulders and forearms sore and heated. Two feelings I hated above all else, unless the heated feeling came from tabasco sauce.

"OK, we'll take it easy with the free weights for now," she said apologetically and put them away. She then led me to where most of the men were, at the machine weights. Amber told me their names, but I can't precisely recall them all exactly. There were benches where two men would help one another raise a metal bar with huge weights the shape of wheels above their chests. Amber said those were bench presses and that they worked the arms and chest a great degree. The man standing idly by was the spotter. His job was to assist the man on the bench if the weight ever became a bit too much for him to handle any further. From what I saw, most of the men were capable of pushing it up over 20 times apiece, at least on average. An average I would bring down fairly soon.

The next machine she led me to looked like something I would enjoy. It was one where the men sat down on a stool of a bench and yank down on a pair of handles. As they leaned forward, they would lift a set number of weights, set total weight. The man we were watching was closer to my size than most, but his muscles were in places where I had nothing but fatty tissue, as Dr. Celso described so pleasantly.

"This machine is perfect for you," Amber said. "It works your back, chest, arms, and stomach all at once. You would be able to convert all the mass you have into solid muscle in no time flat."

"I see." Your body sort of acts as both a lever and a pulley. Your force resistance against your muscles in those four areas in order to increase the amount of work the muscles would exert in order to build themselves up. Amber was right, this machine was definitely for me.

"Would you like to start here or with the treadmill?"

"Let's stay here first," I said. I started walking toward one of the open devices, but then Amber grabbed me by my hand.

"Not so fast, there, Jack. You still have one manner of business to attend to before you can start to utilize this facility fully."

I was perplexed. "What's that?"

She led me into the office and we sat there, across the desk from a sharply dressed young man. He was covered from head to toe with the pristine clothing. His suit was a polished shade of midnight, he had on a white velvet shirt, orange tinted shades, a fuzzy hairdo, and the watch on his hand was copper, but polished so furiously it looked to be gold.

"I'm Andrew," he said. "Andrew Whips. How may I help you to-day?"

"My friend here would like to join the gym as a member," Amber said on my behalf.

"I see. And which membership level would he desire? Basic? Super? Premium?"

"Why don't you describe the differences to him and then he'll decide." Amber said so "he'll decide", but I had the feeling she was going to answer that question, too. And I was fine with that. I didn't know how this type of establishment ran.

"Basic is about $18.99 a month, and it allows you three days a week to come and work out as long as you wish, but no coming in on 10 pm Monday night and staying over until Tuesday at 1am and thinking that counts as one day, that's two," Andrew said. "A super membership means that you can come five days a week and also grants you access to or pool area. The price of that will be $27.99 a month."

No, thank you. I was not going to perpetuate that whale joke by diving into a pool with a bunch of cocky,well muscled strangers. It'd be like serving myself up to a pool full of Harrisons, sharks they would be, and I would be the bleeding dolphin that unfortunately crossed into their domain.

"The premium membership includes everything I've already mentioned, but it's good for each day of the week. The price extends to $45.99 a month and it also means that you will be award a premium ID card, which entitles you to first access to the showers during closing time if you chose to do so. And yes, our showers are communal."

"You mean for both men and women?" I asked without thinking. Amber giggled at my left.

Andrew looked appalled by my question. "No, sir. We have gender specific communal showers." He turned back to Amber. "So, which one would he like?"

"Let's start him on a basic membership, Drew," Amber replied. The way she said Drew was an indicator that they knew each other for some time, which made sense. Amber was a fit woman, and I doubted that she maintained that on her own efforts. I had seen the people lobbying for my mother's property on one of the first days, and she was swamped. This must serve for her as a stress relieving recreational activity, as well to stay in shape.

"All right. I just need you, um…"

"Jack," I filled him in.

"Jack. To fill these forms out and then make a security deposit of $55.00 dollars, as well as your first month's payment of $18.99." He handed me the form and it was all pretty standard stuff on an application. Date of birth, name, address, social security number, blah, blah, blah. I filled it out as quickly as I could, paid him the amount in cash. I was a little sore about that price, though. Why on earth would a gym need a security deposit? Whatever, it was done and over with and I could now hit up that machine from earlier.

I slowly and cautiously sat down on the stool-bench and grabbed at the handle bars. I slowly pulled down, but I didn't feel anything. I smiled and then kept pulling, easing back, and pulling even more. I froze upon the rising of the familiar giggle. I looked up and saw Amber trying not to lose control, holding her sides firmly.

"What's wrong?" I asked.

"You're not really lifting anything," she said in between slips of laughter.

"What do you mean?" I turned around and saw that the pin was free, not placed beneath any of the weights, My cheeks flushed and I tried not to look directly at Amber, but I needed advice. "How does this work?"

"Here, let me show you." She pushed me to the side and then placed the pin beneath 100 lbs and began to pull the handlebars down over her head. Well, I'm sure she was. Her back was sloped so low that I couldn't believe otherwise. Her back arched so perfectly, all the way down to her bottom. It was so tight and…

"Jack," she said all of a sudden. The urgency in her voice made me think that she'd been calling at me for a few seconds there before I snapped back to attention.

"Huh?"

"I asked if you'd like to try. And also, six."

Damn, I was hoping I was being sneakier today. "Sure, I'll give it another go." I took her place and moved the pin to between 60 and 80 lbs. I was going to need to take this slowly.

I began to do what Amber referred to as reps, not rapidly at first, but I soon came to learn that long and slow made the heated shoulders and back muscles only ache worse. By the time I picked up pace, I had lost sight of Amber. I had no clue where she was, but I couldn't focus on her right now. If I stopped now, I wouldn't be able to continue any further. I kept count of the reps I was doing, and I was closing in on around 44…45. I kept going until I hit 60 and then the soreness in my shoulders was not going to permit me to progress anymore. I slowed and then stopped abruptly. I rubbed my shoulders fiercely, trying to ease away the soreness.

I leaned back and sat up straight. My shoulders were still in pain all up until the moment I finally spotted Amber again. She was doing pull ups off on a wall to my right. A pole was raised between two pillars and she gripped her fists around it tightly, the veins in her pals pressing against the skin. The same rang true for her arms as she lifted her head up above the bar. But again, her head was not where my focus was. Each time she rose, I was focused on her chest. As it went up and down, so did my eyes, and probably my whole head. My peripheral vision was kind of shoddy.

"Hey," called out a male voice, resonating somewhere from my peripheral blindspot. IO turned and saw this tall, hulking, shirtless man advancing toward me. His body was as chiseled as the statue from the museum. In fact, this guy was so toned that he could've served in place of that statue on the days they needed it to be stored away for inspections of quality. He had on red sweatpants with the words "Van Nuys Wolves" written on them. Something told me he was not a high school student, though.

"Hey," I said back plainly.

He squatted down beside me and whispered "Don't let Drew catch you ogling the female gym patrons. He'll have you thrown out for that."

"No problem. Thanks for the heads up," I said. And now I know why Andrew gave me that look from before. He probably had me pinged for a pervert from the moment that question escaped my lips. Unless he had too caught my sideways leers at Amber's body. If he had, then my question may have cemented his suspicions then and there.

"So, what's your name, new guy?" the shirtless man asked.

"I'm Jack. And yourself?"

"You can just call me Guns. As you can see, I got two big ones right here," he said in a mocking tone. He lifted his arms and bulged the muscles so tightly that I thought they might burst. He laughed. "But in all seriousness, I'm Riley."

"Nice to meet you, Riley."

We shook hands.

"Anyway, I saw you finishing off your set. It's better if you start *and* end slowly. If you just cut out of the workout, you're not giving your muscles enough time to adjust to the cease in action, and that could lead to knots in your muscles, and that leads to surgery."

"Again, thanks for the heads up. It was actually a trip to the hospital that led me here. I'd hate for this place to be the reason I went back."

"Well, just stick with me and I'll get you looking like me before long," Riley boasted. He may not be in high school, but he definitely had that jock attitude. The only difference was he was nice when he was arrogant. The ones I'd encountered up until now had just been jerks of the highest order.

Riley picked me away from the machine I was on and brought me over to one that looked like one of those massage chairs in the mall, except it only had platforms for your arms to rest on. He told me to sit down and to grab the thin handles protruding from the platforms.

"What this machine does is work your chest and back. You pull your arms in and it constricts the muscles in your chest together, but forces the muscles in your back to spread. In the process, they can grow and gain even more muscle over a wider section of your body. Give it a shot."

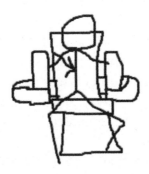

I started out slowly just as Riley instructed. I observed his approving nod as he stood, watching. I could feel the heat starting to boil beneath my flesh, but I could ignore it right now.

"So, Riley, which sport did you play in high school?"

"I played football. Tight end."

"Excuse me?" Was he ogling some poor woman now.

"Tight end. It's a defensive position in football," he clarified and I "ah'd". "Did you play any sports?"

"Not even a little. I used to enjoy tennis, but that was before my gym teacher made us do singles. With doubles, I could slyly let my partner do all the work."

Riley laughed. "I did the same thing. I despised tennis. I used to hate football, too. I could never understand the game when I watched it on tv."

"Then why do you play?"

"Oh, my dad had always wanted to be a football star when he was growing up. He was on his way when his ankles caved on him. He'd always resented that turn of events." Riley turned away for a second and took a breath. "He passed two years ago and never even got to see me win my senior year homecoming game. He would've been proud. I don't play anymore, but I coach a little league team."

"Is it because of your father that you coach?"

"Yeah, I guess. I hope that one or more of the kids I teach will be able to make my father's dream come true. It's my own little way of honoring his memory."

That honoring memories thing is pretty big around these parts I suppose. "Well, I'm sure he's proud of you wherever he is right now." I didn't believe that, but I felt the lie was necessary.

"Thanks, man," Riley said. "Hey, when you're done here, come find me. We could have dinner together."

"Oh, I would, but I've been given a strict diet that I can't stray from," I replied.

"Well, why start today?" Riley asked. "I mean, diets are for regulating your health. Why not start when your week usually begins. Which day of the weak if first for you?"

It made enough sense to me. "I begin my weeks on Monday." I wanted one other day of guilt-free eating before assigning myself to that stupid health regimen.

"Then let's go out tonight. You can even invite your girlfriend." He pointed to my left and when I turned, Amber was standing right beside me. I didn't know for how long. "Catch ya later, Jack."

I looked up at Amber and she gave me a sassy look back. "I can explain."

"It's fine, Jack. Riley's actually right. You should start slowly. No need to force this new life on yourself all at once. Take the necessary time and use it to adjust to this lifestyle. You're already doing excellent by simply coming here and putting in the work," she said.

"But the doctor was strict about sticking to the diet."

"Well, of course. He's a doctor. He has to be strict with his patients about their health. He doesn't want to see you in that hospital every time he walks down to the lobby."

"Oh."

"So, what exercise are you gonna do next? Wanna try pull ups?"

I shook my head vehemently. I could barely lift 100 lbs, so I knew trying my 300 plus was impossible at the moment.

Amber and Riley took turns taking me to all kinds of sections of the gym. From free weights to the tread mills. The free weights were my worst nightmare. I couldn't breathe too well when we finished up there with two sets of 15 curls. I guilted them into letting me catch my breath before we attempted running for twenty minutes straight.

I urged myself to press forward, no matter how fast they made the treadmill go. I made my plea for them to stop when they settled at 3.6 speed. It was worse because they had forced me to incline the treads at a slight angle to simulate running uphill. I was glad that this was the last thing we were going to do. If my body needed food, it was going to need it immediately after the shower I planned on taking.

In the communal shower, I waited until everyone had gone in and come out, even Riley. He was nice, but I didn't want to push to see how nice he could be just yet. I went in, stripped down, and looked appalled by how I looked naked. I never had to see my naked self in my apartment because the bathroom mirror was always too fogged up by the time I was done. Here, the steam was n't nearly enough to reach the mirrors. I saw the folds of my stomach, the lip that poured over my waist, which hid my genitalia nicely. That was something I didn't want to see.

I exited the showers and found Amber and Riley chatting with Andrew near the exit. They were sharing a good laugh, but I tried to shake the thought that it was about me.

"Ah, there's our new trooper," Andrew said when I joined them. "Good first day, champ."

"Thank you," I replied. "I'm oddly looking forward to tomorrow." And that was somewhat true. I now had a place where I could talk to people. And you know what they say, new is always better.

"Well, good to have you." He patted my arm playfully. "Amber. Riley. I'll catch you later." He nodded his farewell.

"See yah, Drew," Riley said.

"Bye," Amber mumbled.

Amber gave me a look that screamed surprise. "Looking forward to tomorrow? Wow. I never thought you'd say that on day one."

"Probably cuz we went easy on him," Riley commented.

My turn to be surprised. "This was easy?"

They both laughed as they led me out of the gym.

"Seriously, this was an easy day?"

I was aghast. I was giving it more or less, everything I had today, and it was only meant to be an introductory course. Was this some prerequisite? Is that why there are super and premium memberships? To give people goals to strive to work toward. How could I even attempt to make it to the super membership? If I had to go through three days of this, how was I supposed to live? My body wasn't ready, but I guess every greenhorn gym patron thinks that at one point, or was it just me?

The restaurant we went to was a sports bar. Riley asked if we could get a table in the bar area. We all sat in a booth nestled between two regular sized televisions and one large one overlooking the bar counter. I didn't recognize any of the team colors, just that it was football. I bet Riley knew.

"Hey, Riley, who's playing?"

"Oh, it's the 49ers and the Seahawks," he said coolly. "I had a roommate in college who said he was going to tryout for the Seahawks."

"How'd he do?" Amber asked, jumping into the conversation.

"I don't know. That's all he talked about the entire time we lived together. I'm sure he at least gave it his best shot."

"What was his name?" I asked.

"His first name was Logan. He seemed older than he looked though. Wicked sideburns. Kind of spacey whenever I asked about where he came from."

"Logan, huh." I liked the way that name sounded. If I ever had a son, he might enjoy a name like that.

Our drinks and food had come and we all sort of sampled each other's dishes. All of us were painfully indecisive about what to eat, so we ordered three things each of us would like, and then split it amongst us. We all ate a third of a bacon cheeseburger, a third of a grilled salmon and about one-third of alfredo linguini pasta. All three portions were amazing, but Riley said he was suffering from an upset stomach and hurried to the restroom. And I don't blame him. My stomach was twisting in knots, too, but Amber assured me it was just my stomach muscles tightening.

While Riley was gone, Amber had crossed over to my side of the booth to watch the game with me. She said the tv she was watching was starting to skip and lag. I wasn't going to call her on it, especially not after she nestled up closer to me, leaning her head on my shoulder, or close enough to my shoulder.

"What do you think actually seahawks look like?" she asked.

"Those are a real thing?"

"Well, they had to get the name from somewhere."

"Maybe they just saw a hawk flying in the air, but they were at sea when they saw it."

"Or maybe they got the name from some foreign land. Maybe Africa has some seahawks? Or perhaps Australia? I mean, Australia has everything."

"Here's hoping that they're alive and well somewhere." I raised my glass and Amber did the same. We clinked them together and sipped, but never once did we break eye contact until we both swallowed. But we immediately locked gazes the second "ah'd".

I'm not sure why or for what reason this next thing happened, but

we both leaned in closer to each other. I had to stop short or risk pushing her out of the booth, so she came the rest of the way and kissed
me. Now, I had never kissed a girl before, but I was now even more
jealous of Harrison from back then. If all those girls fawning over him
gave him this sensation, then he was luckier than I ever imagined.

Her warm, wet lips touched mine and I could taste the beer on her
tongue when it slipped between my teeth like a buttery piece of pancake sliding down my gullet. This was something I could get used to,
and love getting used to it, unlike the diet and the gym, but I wasn't
thinking about those anymore. She pulled away and smiled. I wasn't
sure if she was holding back laughter or if she was sincerely pleased
with my performance.

"We'll have to do that again when I'm not already beat from a workout," she said after a painfully extended period of silence- three or four
seconds.

"I'll look forward to it."

Riley returned a few moments later and we then paid the bill and
left. We hoarded into Amber's van and headed to drop off Riley first.

"Man, I'm not sure what was in that food, but I'm so against going
there again," Riley said.

"Seconded," I said. I was fond of the waiter, Bill. He was needlessly
pushy about orders when the whole restaurant was lax. There weren't
crowded areas, or huge crowds of people waiting for tables, so my
guess was that he was in a point in his life he hated. I sympathized
with that, but I never made other people miserable just because I was.
Devon was the one exception, but she started it.

"Noted," Amber said, but I had a suspicion about who that was
geared toward.

"Was I thinking out loud again?" I asked.

"Oh, yeah," Riley said with a bellowing voice.

"Don't worry, Riley. You'll get used to that. He does it often."

"Until recently, no one ever paid attention to it though."

Amber stopped at a red light. "What can I say, Jack? I just notice
those things about you," she said with a hint of flirtatiousness. Riley
must have picked up on it because he slowly turned his head to me
and then gave me an approving smile. My peripherals weren't too
good, but I could still tell that Amber was smiling. She could read me,

but I was learning to read her, too.

I'm not exactly certain how or when it happened, but the three of us had become buddies practically overnight. It was a pleasant transition. My life before had been as this crippling lonely guy who worked in the back kitchen of a coffee shop. I was eating myself to my doom with one tv dinner after the other. It took my mother dying and my own near death experience to bring me back to my senses. The same sense I had back when I was still friends with Steve had since the diluted themselves to the point that I didn't give one shred of care for my own health. What I didn't realize is that with my withdrawal, I had failed to see any warning signs of my mother's own failing health. From the moment that she had passed, I thought that maybe I could avoid any guilt by simply saying that it could've happened regardless of what I did for her. I wasn't a doctor, but i did know how to find them. When it came down to saving my own hide, I knew what to do, and it only took the time to dial three little numbers. And when I awoke, I was being thrusted on the right path again, my senses sharpening quicker than they ever had before. Thanks to Dr. Celso, Amber, and Riley, and I guess, Andrew, I was going to pull through. It was because of them that I was now back in good spirits, but I was going to work to keep them up by making sure my mother and father could occupy the ground without me for the next few decades. Dozens of decades, if I could miraculously make it that long, but I wasn't fooling myself. And so, with a renewed heart and spirit, I was going to up my timetable. I wasn't starting my week on Monday like I normally did, but I was going to start it on Sunday, the day my father claimed came first.

CHAPTER 7
Short term glory

Short term glory. That's the term I'd used to determine this part of my life. Wl, glory could replaced with a number of other words: happiness, joy, serenity, other positive sounding nouns. It's not like I wanted the happiness to end, it just sort of faded through a long time period of horrible events. It started this morning, a year after I'd started hanging around with Riley and Amber. The unraveling of my world began with a news program.

Not too long ago, I contemplated giving some of my mother's insurance money away to one of the African charities that the news channels scrolled at the bottom of the screen every morning. I'd forgotten about that quest when I started dating Amber, but here it was, and I scrambled to grab a pen and paper. I barely got back to the tv in time to scribble down one of the last charities they promoted. I was going to make some inquiries to them fairly soon.

I figured an annual donation of around $500 was good enough for them. I mean, it was probably more than most, but certainly not the best one-time-a-year donation. I'm sure those rare moments when the wealthy bestow a fraction of their riches to the needy blew my meager contribution out of the water.

I would give the charity a call later, but today, I was hoping to expand upon my super membership at Neptune Fitness. Today, I was going to make the leap to premium. Now, I had not been losing fat, but I had started to get used to the pattern. Workout about two to three hours everyday. I was still the same size, but I was getting better at working the machines and the free weights. The treadmill at a certain elevation was still my worst enemy, but I'd overcome that hurdle one day, well, I was sure I would, until I made a quick stop at the bank.

I tried to replenish the supplies for my diet, but the grocery store said my card was declined, and that shouldn't be correct. I had them swipe a few more times, but with the line growing, along with the hostility of the other patrons, I took my card, returned my groceries, and then headed straight to the source.

I was speechless to learn that both my checkings and savings had been ravaged by the enormity of the gym membership fees. I forgot that I'd made the payments automatic, and neglected to put those into account when budgeting. I had many other bills to attend to, so in the one year time span, I had spent over $700 more dollars than I made room for. I was broke, and to make matters worse, I was jobless and rent was due in two weeks. No way I was going to make that.

I left the bank and sat in my car. I left the engine off. At this point, I needed to pinch as many pennies as I could. If I could, I'd traverse entire highways just picking up the loose change that some people tossed out of their car windows sometimes.

I stayed in the bank's parking lot, silent for about two hours, not sure what I had to do to make ends meet. The only people I could reach out to were just as strapped for cash as me. Riley was in the middle of paying off his college bills and Amber, as good as a real estate agent she was, was actually funding her mother's stay in a home for the mentally ill. I think her mother had dissociative identity disorder or something along those lines. It had to do with identity. But, still, maybe she would understand the situation.

I went home and dialed her immediately. She answered straight away. "Hey, Ames," I said. That was my pet name for her. Hers for me was Jackie.

"Hey, Jackie," she said sweetly. "I didn't think I'd hear from you until later. What's up?"

"I'm quitting the gym." My words must've shocked her, because the net few minutes were silent. "Ames, you there?"

"Why?"

"I've spent a year of my life there, and it hasn't produced the results

I hoped and, to be honest, for the price it's charging, I don't feel that it's worth it."

"If it's a money thing, I can spot you for a few months. My mother's care facility has recently been granted with an anonymous, and large grant, so they price there has halved. I don't think you should halt your progress just yet. Just-"

"Give it time?" I asked, but I knew that's what she planned to say. "I've given it a year, Ames. Nothing's happened to think the gym's been helpful. But, I do need a small loan. I was careless with my gym membership bills, and I've run nearly bankrupt on cash."

There was a pause.

"Um, sure, how much do you need? I can spare up to $650 right now," she stated.

"No, that's perfect, Ames. Thank you. And I'm sorry for springing this on you so suddenly. I've been wracking my brain on what to do for the past two hours and I didn't think of anything, so I had to rely on you."

"Hey, hey, Jack, it's OK. You can always rely on me. There's no request of yours that I'd ever turn down or away unless I felt I couldn't truly do it. Money is no issue for me. I can support you until you find a job. But, just promise me that you'll look really hard. OK?"

"Not a problem. I'll start looking today." I looked down at the charity number. I thought for a moment that just maybe they could have needs for volunteers or employees. It was a long shot, but right now, it was just as good an option as anything. "Hey, call me when you're done for today. I need to run something by you in person."

"That's fine. I'll see you later, Jackie." She hung up immediately like she always did. It was a nice little quirk. I'd hated being on the phone with people who refused to hang up first because they thought it was rude. I wasn't that way, and I was pleased to learn that neither was Amber. Riley didn't call much on phones, or even answer his most times, so I was unsure where he stood on that scale. I'd call him later to try and find out.

I called the number of the African charity. It was called A Can for Africa, A Can for Everyone. It was a mentoring/food providing service for the hungry young men and women in the jungle. And I was right, they were looking for employees. It was a non-profit organization, but there were many benefits that I could make use of to continue my diet. I wasn't going to stop that right away. I was going to follow Riley's advice and slow down my body to get it adjusted to the coming change. There were many dishes in Africa- I assumed- that would contain the three staples that Dr. Celso said I needed more of.

It took three tries, but someone finally answered on the other end. It was a man with a gruff, deep voice. He was the kind of man they'd have guarding prison cells in movies. "Hi, I'm looking to speak with the coordinator for A Can for Africa, A Can for Everyone," I said into the phone.

"What's your name?" the gruff voice asked.

"I'm Jack Garbarino."

"One second, Mr. Garbarino." He kept the phone in hand, but not near his mouth. I couldn't hear him breathing, but I did hear the laughter of jungle children as they ran past, or we ran past them. I could hear other fain conversations, some of which were about food rations and education. I guess mentoring did include furthering the jungle children's learning.

Abruptly, there was a lot of harsh, cutting noise. It was like he'd swatted through a curtain with rings that raked against the metal pole holding them up. There was a swat, a clap, and then another voice, a different man than the one that answered.

"Hello?" This voice was more soothing, more calm. "How may I help you, um…"

"Mr. Garbarino," I heard the first man say.

"Mr. Garbarino."

"I'm looking to volunteer, sir."

"Um, that's very noble of you, Mr. Garbarino, but we're not an organization based in the United States. We operate directly from Africa. Unless you're sure you can move out here, then we have no use for you, I'm afraid."

"Give me a week," I blurted.

"A week to do what, exactly, Mr. Garbarino? Certainly you can't just uproot yourself and fly all the way to Africa to work for us." The man on the other end had a right to be skeptical. He'd probably received many calls of people hoping to volunteer, but that were plagued by the notion of actually making physical contact with third world children.

"Right now, I'm jobless, no college or schooling to hold me back, and I'm unattached." Two out of three truths was good enough. I was planning to speak with Amber about this later, anyway. Now I'd have a real reason to have to inform her about my decision. We would either end our relationship in the coming days, or it would continue as a long distance affair, one of extremely long distance.

There was a pause on the other line, but I could hear breathing, so the man was mulling over my proposal. "And you say you'd only need a week, correct?"

"Just to be safe, let's make it two weeks, but I do plan on being available to fly out there in the next week. All I'd need from you is an address so I can book a flight promptly."

"Mr. Garbarino, I want you to give me a call just as soon as you're sure of your arrival time, and I'll gladly give you the address of the airport you'll need to touch down at. Looking forward to that call."

He hung up.

So was I, but the first thing I needed to do was somehow convince Amber that this was the best move for me. It was sudden, as the man on the other line described, but it was something I'd planned to do since before Amber and I became a couple. I'm positive I'd mentioned it to her at one point or another. My fleeting, background dream of helping the jungle children.

It was about 6:30 pm when she came a knocking at my door. I invited her inside and led her to our loveseat couch. This one was decorated with a beautiful blue and violet floral pattern. It clashed with the rest of the beige and brown apartment, according to Amber, but we both didn't seem to mind that very much. It only costs us $22 at this thrift store in Sun Valley, California.

"So, what's up, Jackie?" She sat beside me and swung her legs over my lap, dangling her feet over the arm of the couch. I grabbed at her feet and began giving her a soft massage. I could tell she was in need of it. I bet she'd been showing other homes today and was walking all over, never stopping to take a break.

"What would you say if I was thinking of joining a non-profit organization that helps young men and women in Africa?"

"I'd say that's amazing. You've mentioned how you wanted to after your mother had passed. I'd gladly support you if that's what you chose to do."

"What if the group was based out in Africa?" I shut my eyes and awaited a verbal lashing unlike any other, but nothing came. Not a shout. Not a threat. Not even a little whimper of a gasp. She was silent. I opened my eyes and faced her. She was smiling.

"I already told you, Jackie. I've always got your back. If you chose to go to Asia to help a panda with a thorn in its paw, I'd back you up. If you think you're flying off to Africa without me, you're dumber than you look."

"But what about your mother?" I asked.

"Look, the funds that go into her care are handled through an escrow account.. I simply just funnel in the resources from time to time."

"And your job as a real estate agent?"

"I can sell homes anywhere. Even in Africa."

"And you're sure about this? Ames, you don't have to come just because I'm going. I'd be OK if you chose to stay here."

"I wish it was all about you, but the truth is, I've fallen into this deplorable comfortability with life. I've got my dream job, a great man, and good friends. I didn't want any of that until I was much older, much wiser and less likely to want to sow my wild oats. But here I am, a 24 year old, dating a 21 year-old, holding her own in a tough career, and making merriment with you and Riley, and my other friends and co-workers. I didn't want any of that until I was in my thirties."

"Still, I want you to know, there's plenty here you'd have to take care of. I'm not as tied down to this place as you are. I'm planning on flying out there just as soon as I can. I wanted to know if you were OK with that."

She swallowed and bit her lip before saying "How soon?"

"I talked to the director earlier today. He said that he'd want me there as soon as possible. I told him I could make it there as early as this week, but as late as next week."

"And what did you tell him?"

"I told him that I'd think over my time tables before confirming when I'd be arriving. I didn't bring you up, but I wanted to hear what your thoughts on this were before I made a final decision."

"To be honest, Jackie, I'm kind of surprised at how long it took you to consider doing this in the first place. You talked about the charity more than you realize, and not just when you do that speaking-out-loud thing that you do. In your sleep, you would sometimes mutter "Africa" over and over. It was cute to have such an undying dream of something that pure and honest. It's a calling I don't share, but it's one I admire nonetheless."

"So, when do you want me to leave? Whatever you choose, I'll stick with."

"In all seriousness, I don't want you to leave at all. But, I know how precious this is to you. Whatever motives are driving this decision, it's for you and I'm not going to stand in your way. I want you to go this week if you want."

"I can wait the extra week. I'd still need to get the proper vaccinations for the trip, and rushing that doctor's appointment this short a notice might not work well with Dr. Celso's schedule."

"When would you want me to come out there?"

"At the earliest point that you could. I'd wait for you even if it took ten years," I said confidently.

"I think I can get all the necessary preparations done in just over a year, maybe a year and a half."

"That's not that bad."

"But," she said curtly.

"But?"

"If I do this with you, Jack, I don't want you to toss me aside for this dream. I know it's something you've wanted for years, but I want you, and I don't want to be your consolation prize. I want a wedding. That's my price. We go to Africa, we get married. Simple as that."

"Of course." I leaned in and stroked her neck so her lips would fit perfectly against my own. We kissed several times before we both pulled away at the same time. "I love you, Ames. If you want a wedding, I'll give you a wedding that 1,000 other weddings couldn't compare to."

"Make it 2,000 and you've got yourself a deal," she teased flirtatiously.

"3,000 may not seem up to par, either," I teased back. We kissed and I led her back to my bedroom.

This wasn't our first time, it was closer to our twenty-first. Our first time had gone so horribly that I wasn't sure we should have counted it, bt Amber said we did the deed in the technical sense, so it counted. Amber and I were still fresh into dating one another and some taunting remarks made by Riley about how slow we seemed to be moving dared s to take a few leaps.

We went back to her place and began to disrobe in her room. I was nervous about being shirtless, but Amber forced me to comply. In comparison, her chest was perfectly sculpted, like some master artists had molded her figure just for me. However, some blind sculptor with four fingers in total had made me for her. She said she didn't mind, but I'll always have my doubts. We meshed together fairly well, but it had been my first time, and I needed much instruction. She obliged, but at a certain point, being told how to exactly do certain actions only made it too awkward to continue.

Every time after that was greater by a significant degree, and she was not shy about showing my gratitude with gifts and *gifts*. Tonight was just another of those times where I would receive a gift.

In the morning, I had awoken to find her still asleep, nestled underneath my arm as the little spoon. I lifted my arm and gently stroked her hair from her face. I couldn't believe how devoted this woman, beautiful as she was, who could have anyone better suited for her than me, still chose to stand by me, even though I'd be moving to another continent, an ocean away. I had to make a promise to her, but after I made one to myself first.

I sometimes recalled the pain I felt when I realized that Steve and I would no longer stay friends, that summer when my calls went unanswered and unreturned. I put on a brave face and pretended around my mother that it didn't bother me as much as I thought, when in truth, it bothered twice as much as I thought. I vowed to myself, watching her sleep so soundly, that I would never invade her with nightmares that she'd been burned by a man who had once proclaimed love for her.

I was in the kitchen making us a breakfast of oatmeal, soy milk, some oranges (sliced into four pieces), and turkey bacon grilled to a crisp. She wandered in, half dressed but still looked ready for a day of showing clients to her company's properties.

"Is this all for us?" she said, amazed. "It looks fantastic."

"Of course it does. My mother didn't teach me how to cook lousy looking food," I boasted with pride.

"Let's hope it's not lousy tasting," she joked. I laughed.

In the past, that comment would have sent me into a rage where my cheeks would puff and my eyes would narrow. But Amber taught me one thing in our year together, well, one thing out of many, and that was to laugh about things in the past. It did no good to sadden yourself with things that were beyond your control, so use them to bring joy to your life instead. It took some time but eventually I'd begun making jokes about her ill mother like she made jokes about my deceased one.

"Try it." I jammed a fork into some of the oatmeal and fed it to her. Her mouth twisted with pleasure, followed by a long "mrmmmm" from her throat.

"Oh, my God, that's frickin' delicious," she exclaimed. "Your mother was an amazing teacher. I take back what I said."

"Thank you. I used to be pretty good at making pancakes, but lately, I just can't seem to stick that first flip too well."

"The first flip?"

"Yeah, my mother said that the first flip of a pancake after the batter's been poured into the pan was critical. If the flip was sloppy or lopsided, the pancake would suffer for it. Not in tastes unless you burned it, too, but it would suffer in its presentation."

"Wow, you're just the encyclopedia of breakfast foods today," she noted. "What's gotten into you?"

"I didn't cook for my mother a lot growing up, even though she did for me. A lot."

Amber turned and faced me with a somber expression, patiently waiting as I told my story.

"I thought i loved her, in fact, I'm sure that I did, but I didn't show her too often. I didn't cook for her, wash her clothes for her just for the heck of it, helped her garden, or even once washed the dishes when I knew she was tired beyond belief."

"Jack..." Amber grasped my hand inside of her own.

I laid my left hand on top of hers. "I went through one life without ever showing her any love, but I won't do the same with yours. I love you, Amber, and I want you to know that I'm not going to treat you any less than the love of my life, even though we'll be an ocean apart for a while. You'll be my number one for years and years to come."

We had a ten year time bomb that set for us the moment I said that, but again, that's getting ahead of things. Plenty to cover between now and then.

"The point is, Amber, I don't want you to worry for even a second that I'll one day not answer the phone because I was with another woman, or because I was tired of waiting for you, or anything like that. If I don't answer the phone, you'd better believe that I'll call you right back."

She smiled and blinked as tears made a beeline for her chin.

I took her face in my hands and kissed her once more, and again, and again until the salt of her tears had touched my lips, too. "I love you," I whispered.

"I love you, too," she whispered back.

We spent the next week, just the two of us, in happy bliss. It was filled with many late night chats and trysts, along with a few tear eyed embraces. We saw Riley a few times, but mainly in passing. He still went to the gym, but had downgraded back to a basic membership since his college tuition was only increasing more and more.

The day of my departure was a day away, so today was meant for the vaccinations against the known African diseases that could plague an American citizen. Amber took me to see Dr. Celso who was some-how able to tell my fatty tissue had decreased somewhat since the diet and exercise regimen began.

"My, my, Mr. Garbarino. You've certainly reached a new level of discipline," he complimented.

"Thank you, Dr. Celso," I responded.

"So, it says here that you're in for some routine travel vaccinations. Not a problem." He put down his chart, placed on some rubber gloves, and then withdrew a needle with a specific fluid inside of it. I had to receive four of five vaccinations, and they all had to be administered in the same spot. I dropped my pants, bent over the bench, and waited as he swabbed alcohol over the area and stabbed me with the syringe.

After the somewhat homosexual images of another piercing anoth-er's bottom flashed through my mind, I had a moment of clarity where my mind was clear, blank, empty. I'm not sure what was in those syringes, but I felt a little...well, loopy. It was like my mind floated outside my body to observe and document my trippy state.

"Hey, doc, what's above your head?" I asked in my delirious state.

Dr. Celso and Amber exchanged worried looks. My mind's eye was right to be concerned, too.

"I think he's having one of the rare side effects that the injections sometimes cause," Dr. Celso explained to Amber.

"How long do the side effects typically last?"

"This is my first time seeing a patient suffer from them, but I'd give it no less than half an hour. If the condition persist for more than four hours, consult an anesthesiologist immediately."

"Thanks, Dr. Celso."

He took his leave, but turned and looked back at my out-of-control body stumble around the room, picking through drawers and cabinets. I looked on as Amber had forced me to lay down on the bench, as if I was about to be put into surgery. I know that anesthesiologists have something to do with surgical operations, but that's just my medical know-how failing me once more.

It took nearly two hours, but my mind and body felt like one once again. And damned good thing, too. I was tired of watching my drugged self rummage through unsterilized needles and other pokey doctor's tools, like scalpels. Amber drove me home and put me right to bed. She said "Your flight leaves tomorrow afternoon, so get as much rest as you can. I'll be by at around 3 pm to take you to LAX, so be ready, OK?"

The drugging effect had exhausted me so, so all I could manage to confirm I'd heard her was with a thumbs up.

We were at the airport and Amber helped me unload my other two bags of luggage. We hugged, embraced one another, and then kissed.

"I'll call you the moment I find a phone," I promised her.

"You better mean it, Jackie."

And with that, I went through security, checked my bags in, and boarded my flight, nonstop to Africa. My destination was in South Africa, at the airport called Mossel Bay Airport. The main branch of the organization was based there. I was to meet with the director, Florence Michaels, who was going to tell me where my true assignment was. I'd spoken with him twice on the phone a couple of days ago, and he said there was a school that recently opened in need of hands to rehabilitate jungle children that were found trekking through the brush right outside of town. I didn't have any experience working with feral children, but I was going to find out in over 24 hours once I landed how much of a challenge this part of my life was truly going to be.

CHAPTER 8
Stay out of the brush

The flight was pretty tamed. Nothing too crucial happened there, just some general discomfort, but when a flight lasted almost one full day, it was hard not to experience that.

I found my transportation pretty quickly. Not too many Garbarinos were arriving from America, so that made it simple to find my driver. He was as polite as could be, but his accent made it a little hard to follow his speech.

"Welcome to South Africa, Mr. Garbarino," he said in a droll, drawn out way, like every syllable needed emphasis.

"Thank you for having me," I said. I looked around as he drove me through the crowded airport highways. There were plenty of homes that scaled from the lower parts of hills and into valleys, even up close to the summits of small mountains. It was breathtaking. "It's beautiful here."

"Not as beautiful beyond the brush, though."

"Why's that?"

"Because the brush be filled with many predators that could kill you and I like flies," he said, the droll speak only making the minous feel of his words more frightening. "And I ain't just speaking about the big ones, either. The little ones, even the baboons and the spiders, could do us in."

"Then I'll just stay out of the bush, then."

"Brush," he corrected. He leered at me through the rearview mirror and his cold, intense glare unnerved me more than his story. I looked away and just focused on the scenery, opposite the brush.

My enigmatic chauffeur had reached my hotel as the sun was setting. It was too late tonight, so I would meet with the director, Mr. Michaels, in the early morning. For now, I was going to avoid the smaller creatures, assuming the hotel had flawless security that the big animals could not possibly pass through unnoticed.

My bedroom was pretty amazing compared to my one room apartment back home, which was more of a sad comment on my life. This hotel room was one up to my former living arrangements back home. The sheets were incredibly soft and full, like fluffy clouds made out of wool. The drapes and television were pretty classy, too, as in better than the ones I owned that Amber was taking care of for me. I packed my bags into the closet and then sank on top of my bed sheets, and they felt like the clouds they looked like. I was asleep in no time at all.

The next morning, I had a new chauffeur, this one was lighter skinned, but produced the same accent when he spoke. "Hello, sir. I'll be taking you to see Director Michaels."

"Thank you." I hopped into the car through the door he opened for me. The windows were tinted so I couldn't as easily watch the terrain and buildings flash through my field of vision like I'd hoped.

When we stopped, he opened the door for me again and ushered me toward an office with a white linen doorway. I pushed the linens aside and entered, but my escort stopped there.

At the back of the tent/office, there was director Michaels, working on some paperwork. He fiddled with his glasses, trying to make sense of what I could guess were a series of number, perhaps relating to some sort of budget. I stood in the entryway, arms folded behind my back, just waiting. It took him a few seconds, but he noticed my presence with one quick upward glance. "Ah, yes, Mr. Garbarino. Have a seat."

I walked to the desk and took the chair opposite Mr. Michaels. He was still pressing the issue of the numbers as I patiently waited for him to speak to me again. It took another five minutes or so when he said "Be right with you." I would be inclined to believe him, but it took him so long just to say that one message, ironically.

Another five minutes passed.

"Mr. Michaels?"

He raised up a finger. "Just one second, Mr. Garbarino."

I sucked in a breath for it was all I could do not to yell at this man. I understand that he's busy, but manners were still a thing. At least, I hoped so. My early life had me questioning that law, but somewhere I figured it was true. Now, I wasn't so sure again.

Mr. Michaels flipped the paper over and after he looked it up and down once or twice or thrice, he seemed satisfied, nodded, and then made a little check mark near the top of the page. He placed in a cabinet behind his desk and then clasped his hands beneath his jaw, facing me.

"Sorry, about that, Mr. Garbarino," he said with a half sincere tone. It didn't matter. I was planning on forgetting the waiting never happened and that I'd just now shown up. "How was your flight? Enjoyable? I hope."

"The ride here was much more fun," I said. I didn't get to see much of this nation too much through the half-closed window on my flight, but the drives here in the jeep and the car were both very eye-opening. I got to see so much of this beautiful country already."

"I'm glad you enjoyed yourself. Most first timers only think of how long it'll be before we send them to Cape Cod to see the cannon fire at Noon."

I was stunned. "There's a cannon?"

"Yes," Michaels said dryly. "It's cannon atop a hill in Cape Cod that they fire once a day. They generally don't aim it at anything or anyone, but it's still cool to see."

"I wish I'd researched this place before coming. Knowing that tidbit would've made my first night here something special. Are we close to Cape Cod?"

"Not terribly close nor far, but it could be reached by a few select buses," Michaels answered.

"It would make a good field trip for the children," I stated. And it would. Or was that insensitive? I was not caught up on the history of the cannon.

"I'll keep that in mind for when we have the appropriate funding for such a trip."

"So, Mr. Michaels, where would you like to assign me to work?" I was eager to start inspiring and teaching youths. Oh, wait, teaching. I was finally making some headway on the bet that Steve and I had made all those years ago. Not that I'd have any way of telling him that, but I still felt good about finally being able to teach someone.

"There's a small village, about two towns over. We have a few of our members already stationed there, teaching some of the younger children to speak English and some basic elementary math skills."

"And you want me to go there and help out?"

"Yes, sir. You'd be the fourth member of that particular team. I'll start you out there for two years and see how well you can adjust to this nation's laws and practices. None are more harsh or as unpredictable as that village's."

I was a bit nervous at the mention of unpredictable. "How do you mean?"

"You will find out in due time, but before I forget, we need you to take a photo for an ID badge. You will need it to walk around the village freely without suffering the scrutiny of the village officials. Your other teammates will fill you in once you arrive. Now, follow me."

He stood and led me down toward a sectioned off portion of the tent/office. He shut the curtain behind us and then told me to sit down between two very powerful lights that nearly blinded me when he cut them on. It was like being sandwiched between two white hot suns. My face and forearms seemed to blister lightly due to the close proximity to the heat they were giving off.

"Now, sit still and sit up straight, please, Mr. Garbarino."

This was worse than when I took high school yearbook photos and the photographer would come and physically adjust my posture like I was so horrible looking with slumped shoulders. And that's when Director Michaels came and took his swing at it. He approached me, smiling, as he took a much longer amount of time to try and fix my posture when I realized that I'd spoken out loud again.

"Sorry if anything I said was offensive," I apologized.

"No problem."

Director Michaels took the picture at long last and then had me wait while it printed out. It took several minutes, but I just watched the pink sky slowly regain its natural blue colors as the sunrise was reaching its peak in the sky where it was easily able to tell it was around 9 am.

Director Michaels returned with my ID badge with the initials ACAACE under my name, Jack Garbarino. He'd clipped it onto a lanyard for me and handed it over. I draped it around my neck and I was now officially a member of A Can for Africa, A Can for Everyone.

"Take this with you everywhere. Do not drop it, misplace it, bury it, nothing but keep it with you at all times. Do you understand?" He couldn't have made it sound more urgent.

"Yes, sir," I said.

"Good, you're free to do as you like for the remainder of today. Tomorrow, at 9 am, a driver will take you to the village. Be outside your hotel with all of your belongings by then."

"Got it."

"And last little thing, Mr. Garbarino." His look turned icy, like a lethal, frigid blade ready to pierce any vital part of my flesh, which was anywhere, honestly.

I swallowed and awaited his final cryptic warning.

"Stay out of the brush."

I spent the rest of the day wondering just what lied within these forest jungles that seemed so scary to everyone. I mean, I'd watched my fair share of Animal Planet, but it didn't much seem like every inch of Africa was crawling with creatures that could kill you. I mean, I wasn't going stomping through the Serengeti, but to run with lions and hyenas and cheetahs. I was going to let them hunt other slow, rotund beasts. My chances of survival against even solo members of those species was low, but they always seemed to work as units on Animal Planet specials.

I was prepared to leave an hour prior to the scheduled time, so take off was a breeze. The driver and I took very little time in loading my luggage into the trunk, but the road to get to the village was a bumpy one. It was pretty much a straight dirt path with dips and bumps all along the entire stretch of it. My conversation with the driver was a little rough to understand.

"When will we be there?" I asked.

"Before dark," he replied.

"Could you be more specific?"

"Before the stars in the sky become visible," he stated.

"So before dark, then?"

"Yeah."

"Lovely." And all my sarcastic angst was gone.

We reached the village about two hours later. I had fallen asleep at one point, but my body did one of those mind/body splits like it did at Dr. Celso's office. I saw all the scenery that I didn't actually see. I still don't understand how, but it was like a force had lifted me from my body to give me a perspective on my own journey, not retrospective, but current-spective.

The wet jungle leaves and foliage roadways had replaced the incredibly bumpy earthen highway we were on prior. The brush got closer and closer as the road narrowed. We were so tightly packed between the two sides that some of the leaves, mossy with morning dew, would feel like cool slices against my skin, but if heated slices caused pain, cooled ones awarded one a sense of being refreshed. I saw a thin smile dance along my lips momentarily when it happened.

I had been awaken by the driver when we parked near the edge of the village, beside three other jeeps. I was fully rested, so when I peered over and saw firearms stowed in the trunks, I was kind of alarmed. Were there dangerous people out here in the brush, too? Or did they never mean animals to begin with? Were spiders and baboons code names for certain militant groups or something like that?

I dismissed them altogether because thinking about that only put my nerves on hyperdrive, and I wanted to appear calm before my teammates and the jungle children. The last thing I needed was my work here to be ruined by a terrible first impression.

The area was smaller than I expected it bo, but that wasn't necessarily a bad thing. It just meant it was much harder to get lost and accidentally stray from the village. It was practically one huge circle, or perhaps on oval. I'm not sure how to exactly describe the difference between the two of them. Riley used to say that a basketball was a circle and a football was an oval. It made sense, but I still couldn't grasp the idea, strictly on a definition basis.

I found that many things were not as good as I expected them to be. The lodgings were made of bamboo, which was strong, but the bamboo looked as rotten as the tomatoes I would sometimes to forget to eat when I bought them. I thumped the bamboo and it appeared quite solid, scraping my finger in direct opposition to my assault. It looked to be about big enough to house no more than 30-40 persons. If I had to guess, the four drivers, the four members of the ACAACE (which now included myself), the students (the number of which I was never given), and whomever supplied those firearms. I was hoping that I wouldn't have to learn to use one, but given all the cryptic warnings about the brush, I knew I would need to.

My driver and I gathered up my bags and climbed up the stairs to the second floor of the lodgings. To my surprise, the steps didn't creak beneath my weight and I wasn't winded by the time we reached my door. The gym may not have exceeded my expectations, but it at least met the minimum requirement. I could walk up steps without doubling over. It was room 24. I unlocked the door and we dumped my bags near the front door. The driver turned and left in a haste, but that was fine. His role was done for today as far as I knew.

My room was about as good as my apartment back home, and that was fine with me. Pristine and clean was good for most people, but dingy and run down, that's what I was accustomed to, and I didn't want or need anything better.

I had called Amber last night from the hotel room, but due to long distance rates, we kept the call under ten minutes. I told her all about the fancy hotel they'd put me up and we both joked how I must be uncomfortable staying in such a lavish place. I wasn't uncomfortable, but I certainly didn't feel at home there. I felt like I had just joined a club without a single invitation. I was a wedding crasher. I was the guy who shows up late and interrupts an extremely sensitive or crucial moment.

I unpacked my clothes and filed them into my drawers and closet as I deemed fit. The sunglasses that Amber bought me on our way to the airport were resting on top of the bureau. All of my nicer clothes, which meant polos and the three button down shirts I did own, were in the closet. Most of my shirts, t-shirts with graphic art on the fronts or backs or on both sides, along with the multitude of my shorts and plus-sized pants, went in the drawers.

When I was done packing, I was slightly out of breath, but my wits were still intact enough to notice the young lady who stepped into my doorway. Her shirt was dark and had the organization's acronym over her left breast, so I assumed she was one of the teammates. She was petite, even compared to Amber. She had short cut brunette hair, and I would've mistaken her for a boy if she not had breasts. Her arms and legs were little nubs of skin compared to my own, but she looked more muscled and strong than a first glance would warrant. If not for the sun shining through the door, illuminating the minute curves of her biceps and forearms, I might not have noticed either.

"Hi, I'm Jack Garbarino, the new guy," I introduced to her.

"Hi, Jack Garbarino," she said with a youth's innocently shaped voice, like she'd not seen the weapons in the jeeps. "I'm Alexis Jordans, but everyone just calls me Lex."

"Nice to meet you, Lex." I stood and crossed the room to shake her hand. When we were both in the doorway, I could see the faint edges of other, smaller people at her side. All of them were dark-skinned, with dark hair and darker shades of eye colors I'd seen in the States. Not like they all had black eyes, but darker hues of green and brown. Not many cobalt blues, but I think I glanced one or two.

"Are these your students?" I asked.

"Yes, sir," she said. "I teach them math. We've just started to work on multiplication and division."

"Oh, that's wonderful." I turned to the kids. "Do any of you know the answer to five times twelve?"

One of the cobalt blues raised his hand politely and I pointed at him so he could answer. "Sixty," he said.

"That's correct. Good job." I wasn't that good at multiplication at his age, so these kids either had better instructors or were just clearly smarter than me. I gazed into everyone's faces to make sure I hadn't just spoken out loud by accident. I didn't.

"That's Dende," she said. "He's the smartest young man in the village."

"Keep at it, Dende. Being smart is just as important as being strong these days," I told him. And I believed it. I certainly wasn't strong growing up, but I wasn't living up to my fullest academic potential either. I wanted these kids, especially those who had the talent, to succeed in the areas I didn't. Of course, they could succeed in the same subjects I did, too.

"Yes, sir," Dende said. He was actually pretty much me at his age.

Portly, sweet, reserved, and was studious. The only difference we seemed to have was the color of our skin, and I didn't think that made much of a difference, but history books would label me a visionary if I'd be around in the times when Dende's people were shipped overseas to serve my own.

"So, when do I meet my students?" I asked Lex. "Director Michaels was too big on the specifics of the assignment, so I'm a little lost as to what I'm supposed to be doing here."

"Yeah, don't hope for him to get more specific in the future. I've been here three years and what you got is the best any of us should hope to receive. But let me fill in some of the blanks," Lex said. I nodded. "OK, so basically, we all teach the same students, but we trade off on days. I always teach science, but tomorrow, I'll be teaching a different group of students. We have about three groups of students, so until more come arrive, you're going to be helping me out as an aide. Is that fine with you?"

"That shouldn't be an issue."

"Good. We're actually headed to class if you'd like to join us. I know you're still settling in, so you don't have to today." She was kind to extend that offer, but I wasn't going to stall this anymore.

"No, I'll be happy to tag along. No better way to settle in that to just jump right into something," I said with glee. OK, so technically, that was wrong, but there were two sides to my decision. Muscles and exercises were one thing, but new conditions and pools were another. The quickest way to get used to the cold pool water is just to dive all the way right away. I was going to use pool logic here instead of exercise logic.

"So, where's the classroom?"

"Right this way." She turned to the students. "Class, stay in single file and follow behind me and Mr. Garbarino."

"Yes, ma'am," the class sounded off like it was a drilled in response. But I'm guessing there were worse things to drill into children than manners.

We took the students back downstairs and then we crossed the muddy part of the yard. The classrooms were built from the same rotten-looking bamboo as the lodgings, but I'd learned that they just looked that way because of the weather, as Lex explained. I opened the door for Lex and the students to enter. Dende was last, and I knew the look on his face. It was the same one I'd had pasted on whenever I entered classes in middle school. He was trying not to appear vulnerable to insults about his body. And when I saw him sit in the front of the class, similarities between him and I were so crazy that I saw myself sitting in his spot again. I was back in the fifth grade again.

I had just started my first day of fifth grade and it was the day I'd met Harrison. The "Porker" thing hadn't started yet, so he took to calling me,

"Piggy. Hey, piggy. Shouldn't you be at the farm?" he taunted. At first, I hadn't known to him whom he was referring to. Before then, I had not been teased much about my weight. He tapped my shoulder. "Hey, piggy, I'm talking to you."

"What?" I had said. I was confused. I mean, I knew what teasing was back then, but since fat jokes were never aimed at me prior to that, I was understandably naive to what he was doing.

It didn't take long before I caught on and was on the verge of tears daily that he began calling me cry-baby, as well. If it wasn't bad enough, his buddies had joined in on the "fun" soon after. And it wasn't just during school, either. I had to suffer them bullying me on walks to the bus stop. It was crippling, the pain I felt when it first began. In retrospect, I'm more angry at myself that it took over a year to stand up to him.

I looked back up at the front of the class and saw him nervously tapping his pencil against his desk and his foot against the floor. Dende wasn't just dreading the insults, he was expecting him, and his anxiousness was showing. Without even looking, I could see the sharks approaching his beach, slowly but surely, biding their time until the tide could ride them, farther up onto his shore.

Lex wrote a few multiplication problems on the chalkboard and one of them was four times ten. I knew that if any of these kids had met American children before, they'd seize the opportunity to make the joke I felt coming on, and based off of Dende moving the pencil to between his teeth to chew on, they clearly had.

"OK, class, what is four times ten?" Lex asked and scanned the room. She zeroed in on Dende. "Dende, would you come up and answer it, please," she ever so sweetly requested of him. I would say

Dende was lucky, but then I saw that "be nice" plastered on Lex's face for the rest of the class to see. Of course. If Dende saw it coming, Lex would have had to noticed it, too. Guess she was more attentive than chaperones I'd been burdened with in the past. And it meant that Dende had a better safety net for the past three years, assuming that he's been with Lex the entire time. Oh, wait, no, she said that the other two teammates switched classes with her. It made me wonder if all three of them took the same degree of care for Dende. I'd make it my first mission to find out.

Dende wrote "40" beneath the solution line. The kid was correct again. And if you wondering, the word that most other students would have written beneath it would've been portly. It sounded close enough to forty and was a good synonym for the more rotund fellows like Dende and myself. I was astonished that someone like Harrison was able to be so clever. Someone probably figured it out for him.

The rest of the class was pretty standard. Lex reviewed each of the problems and explained why some students answered wrong, reviewed the rules of multiplication to them, and then they were each given a worksheet of multiplication equations to solve. Lex was stern when she gave them a time limit of fifteen minutes. One minute per each equation on the sheet. After handing them out, she joined me in the rear of the room. Probably to chat with me, but I suspected to keep a good eye out for cheaters. It was easier to cheat with the proctor in front of you. But behind you, where your eyes couldn't reach, she could be standing right behind you and you'd never know, unless you had better peripheral vision than me.

"You're a pretty good teacher," I complimented her.

"Thank you," she replied. "I swear though, sometimes these kids are more focused on each other than the work."

"Yeah, but Dende can take it," I said in a hushed voice.

"So, you noticed it, huh?" she asked, also in a hushed tone.

"Well," I patted my belly, "let's just say I know where Dende comes from."

"Ah. I didn't want to assume so, which is why it caught me off guard when you noticed. That, and I don't think the other two members really see what he goes through when the other children bully and poke fun at him."

That answered one of my pressing questions about our other team-mates. I was hoping for better news, but it is what it is. I'm not out to change anyone's views on the subject of elementary school bullying. It's not going to change at any point in the near future. But, I could change this one kid's perception of himself. Amber and Riley had done so for me, and I could do so for Dende. But first, I now had a new question for Lex.

"It sounds like you've been bullied yourself?"

"I was tiny throughout most of my life, still technically am, but it was much worse growing up a good foot shorter than your classmates. It was every bit as daunting as being fat or wearing glasses."

"I can only imagine. I had the good graces to hit my growth spurt before sixth grade. If I hadn't, my tormentors would've had too much ammo. My beach would've been polluted with trash."

She gave me a weird look. "Your beach?"

"It's a metaphor." A private one. I hadn't even shared it with Amber. At least, not as far as I knew. If I had spoken of it out loud one day, she might've simply kept that knowledge to herself.

"Gotcha."

"So, any other kids excelling in math besides Dende? I'm sure there are other little geniuses on the rise in the other two groups," I said.

"Yes and no," Lex answered. "Dende isn't the only one good at math, but he's the only one equally good at everything. Math. Science. English."

"What about history?"

"We don't yet have a teacher for that subject or a fourth group to support that subject. Plus, it'll take some time for the textbooks we ordered to arrive."

"I'd volunteer to teach it if we ever get a fourth group of students," I said. I disliked history most as a child, but I guess it was worth it to know of things that transpired in the past. These kids might even treasure it more than us American born children.

"Do you even know basic American history?"

"Of course I do."

"Who was the twelfth president?"

"Zachary Taylor."

"Who abolished slavery?" she asked quietly.

"Abraham Lincoln," I said just as quietly.

"Which order in the presidential line was he?"

"Fifth."

"Wrong. Sixteenth. You're thinking in terms of money. His face may be on the five dollar bill, but he wasn't the fifth president."

"Well, I got two out of three. On average, I passed, even though it was barely," I admitted.

"Try thumbing through the textbooks when they arrive and then we'll see what you'll be able to do."

We talked for the next ten or so minutes while the kids finished up their assignments. Neither Lex nor I were surprised to learn that Dende was the first to complete his entire sheet. He sat there with his hands clasped together, awaiting his next instruction like a dutiful soldier waiting for his next set of orders. Still, silent, composed. Unlike the rest of the rambunctious group. Restless, noisy, frantic.

Later that day, after classes for the children were over, I was taken into a basement area. I was right with my hunch that firearm proficiency was a requirement here. Lex, along with the other two members, Henry and Nathan, were going to teach me how to shoot. Lex chose my weapon for me, a small, .38 caliber handgun. Henry fied my posture to shoot with and Nathan set up the paper target and supplied everyone with noise-canceling headphones.

My shooting was better than I expected. I'd never once even seen a firearm this close up, but it was some kind of a drug, for certain, the rush of power it shoots through your arms with each shot, it was like being on short-burst steroids. Right after each casing clattered to the ground, I felt like I could punch holes in the walls around us. To call it exhilarating was an understatement.

My hunches, for a second time, were also correct. Baboons were the codename for some loose organized splinter cell roaming the area, but we had guards in place, so I wasn't worried. Spiders, well, that just meant what it meant- deadly spiders did wander into camp from time to time. We didn't have enough ready antivenoms, so we were told to always check clothing thoroughly before getting dressed, shoes and slippers especially. Dark places are their safe havens.

It was dinner time now, and I was sure hungry. I tried not to impose the rush for food since it was still my first day. I was positive that Lex and I hit it off well, but Henry and Nathan were more than standoffish after my poor shooting skills. I'd have to work on those two slowly, but surely.

I would have taken the time at dinner to get to know them better, but then I saw another all too familiar sight, Dende having lunch by himself. Whether it was pity, or because I saw this as a chance to make life better for someone plagued by the same growing pains as me, I couldn't entirely be sure which force drove me to him more. The only thing I knew was that both of us needed. Me, to try and reconcile some flaws I knew I had back then. Him, he just needed someone to lend a friendly ear.

He was so startled when my tray touched down on the table before him. The look he shot me was on of intense fear, but was quickly replaced with a smile. "Hi, Mr. Garbarino."

I wanted to correct him, but his sense of manners was too impressive to try and break down, so I stayed Mr. Garbarino for him. "Hi. You're Dende, right?"

He nodded.

"I saw you in math class today. You were amazing," I said.

"Thanks, I study every day. Ms. Jordans says that a commitment is the strength to increase potential."

I had learned quite a few names today, so it did take me a minute or two to recall that Lex's surname was Jordans. "That's a good quote. I've got one for you, too."

"Should I write it down?" Before I could even answer, he'd already produced a notepad and a pencil. The kid had quick hands. He was awaiting my words.

"OK, well, it's not as much of a quote as it is advice," I corrected myself.

"I'll still write it down. Knowledge recorded is knowledge not forgotten."

"Dende," I took a breath. "As you can see, I am like you in one truly obvious way. We're both very big men Bigger than the kids who tease you. And yes, bigger is better." He caught on to my joke and laughed. He had such a sweet laugh, and I wanted to give him more reason to show it off. "There will always be people around who see the two of us as, well, comic material, but we're much more than that. People like us develop an island. A place no one can penetrate of traverse but ourselves. It's our sole defense, a great defense, though. Each time someone tells you or says something about you that you find annoying or abhorrent, let it flow to your shore, wash up in the tide, and then watch it slide on away. Do you understand?"

"Um," he paused, thinking and reflecting on speech thus far. He was more than smart, he was comprehending, too. You could show this kid a calculus equation and he'd work his mind tired to solve it, but he would definitely solve it. "Is it like that one saying "In one ear, and out the other"? The kid was a genius for sure.

"Exactly," I told him. "But simply ignoring the insults, taunts, and mockeries isn't enough. Having armor is one thing, but having a sword is another entirely. To build yourself up, to strike back at the negative words of others, you only need one word, one prescription to give you a strength they don't possess. It's a thing called self-confidence."

"Self-confidence?" he repeated as a question.

"Yes, self-confidence. The power to know that you're the best you that you can be. The best you that you want to be. Are you what you want to be?" I meant for the question to be rhetorical, but Dende was too devoted. If you gave him a question, he wanted to give you an answer.

"I think I am. What should I want to be?"

And there it was. For all the knowledge and wisdom this kid had, he was still a child. And I wanted him to be a child, so that's what I said.

"Be a child? What does that entail?"

"That means you do your homework, you play with others, you make friends, you fall down, you get hurt, you get better, you grow up, you learn, and you mature. I know it sounds like a lot, but it's the easiest thing you can do for yourself. So, when dinner is over, I want you to find some of the other kids and play a game with them. Do you hear me?"

"Yes, sir," he said after weighing options in his mind. He was still frightened, but I knew he would do it. He was obedient to a fault, but this fault was going to help him become someone I couldn't before I met Amber. Be confident in your skin, and no one can use it against you.

And true to his word, like there was ever a doubt, Dende found a group of other boys from a different group- smart move- and they started talking and Dende was smiling and laughing. I couldn't hear it from here, but his laughter got the other boys into a similar fit and I guess it had an infectious quality to it, too. Lex walked up beside me and nudged my arm with hers in a friendly way.

"Congratulations," she said.

"For what?"

"First, for helping me to win a bet. Henry and Nathan believed that you'd just end up chasing off Dende. I bet that you'd be able to get him to listen. And that leads into our second part, that you were able to get him to talk to another kid. He's been so unfathomably shy that we thought he'd never make a friend." She turned and looked up at me like I held some sort of magical power, a higher ability that she couldn't fathom. "What did you say to him?"

"What I wished someone had told me at his age," I responded.

The week was a glorious time for Dende, I could tell. He'd been playing more often with those same boys he'd talked to after dinner. He had introduced me to them. The taller one with the dark curly locks and emerald eyes was Omar. The shorter one with the eyes a shade lighter than Dende's was Makhaya. They didn't seem at all too muscular either, so I guess Dende found them the least intimidating to approach. I would watch his eyes wander from time to time and he would revere the guards with a sense of apprehension, like they were his enemies.

And Dende wasn't the only one. All the boys, young as they were, saw their protectors as threats, and I couldn't understand why at first, but it sunk in. I grew up in neighborhood where it was dangerous at certain hours of the night. Here, it was dangerous all the time. Weaponry that was wielded in open sight provided less comfort for the children on the camp than it did for me. They might have believed that they were going to be shot without warning. It was a cruel realization, but I couldn't do much there. That was an issue they'd all grown and solidified their responses to long before I came around. Weapons- bad. Hidden weapons- worse. Exposed weapons- the worst of the three.

I adopted their attitudes before long. I would grow wary of a guard marching right outside of the classroom doors while class was being held. A strong military presence in the vicinity of learning was the oxymoron, military-intelligence, personified. It made me feel like these children were being groomed as American allies for what could be future battles on this foreign land. The thought both disgusted and infuriated me.

I had not even spent a month here, and the well-being of this kids was one of my top priorities. Education was the topmost of them, but I couldn't truly mentor these jungle children properly if they weren't having fun, and it didn't appear as if they had any while they were here.

I wanted to sponsor a fun day. Lex told me how to get approval for that with the paperwork and the channel of authority and all that bureaucratic nonsense. The real information I needed was from the jungle children. I needed to know what it was they were starved of. Was it sports? Movies? Video games? I needed to understand what they wanted and how I could go about making sure everyone was happy with my choice.

I got my day approved, but I only had a week to get an idea and plan it and have it. I called the jungle children to the auditorium and gave each of the kids a sheet of paper.

"What I want you all to do with the paper in front of you is simply write one sentence. The only rule is that the sentence has to start with "I really want to" and then the rest is up to you. Write whatever pops into your heads after you recite those words out loud. You have five minutes. Go!"

The off tune chorus of the jungle children's voices reciting "I really want to" was the sweetest thing. I could hear the whimsy in their voices. They knew this had a purpose, and they were going to take advantage of it. And I wanted them to.

They all wrote down their sentences and I collected the papers.

"I'll look these over tonight and tomorrow, based off of the majority of what most of you said, I'll announce the plans for Monday. You're dismissed."

I expected a mass exodus of excited jungle children. What happened had caught me completely off guard. One by one, they came up to me and hugged me. Some of them were crying quietly as they did so.

Were they that drained of fun around here that they would cry joyously at the first sign of it? I'd need to talk to Mr. Michaels about this soon.

I read through the sentences and most of them were pretty much the same, but some were different. I really want to play kickball. I really want to play a game of kickball. I really want to watch a movie. I really want to play with a ball. I really want to see my parents. I really want my mommy. I really want to be like Mr. Garbarino. Something told me that one belonged to Dende, but after the procession of hugs, I couldn't honestly predict that with 100% certainty.

I announced the activity the next day as promised and they all generally seemed to approve of a kickball match. I requested from Mr. Michaels if we could have a bus come and to drive us and the jungle children to the nearest baseball field. He said that it'd be a gigantic pain, but I pushed him on this. I wasn't going to become another disappointment in the eyes of these jungle children. He conceded and on Monday, a few school buses had come to chauffeur us to a baseball diamond. I told the guards to leave the guns behind. I didn't want the day soiled by their gun-toting habits.

The field that Mr. Michaels had been able to rent out was small, but we'd make due. After we got to the field, we split up the teachers as coaches for the separate teams. Lex and I were on one side, Henry and Nathan on the other. We split the jungle children up evenly and then assigned the positions. I placed Dende at home plate, Makhaya at second base, and Omar as our pitcher. I wanted them all lined up in a straight line. They had good communication, so having them cover the center of the infield was a smart choice, something that I know Henry and Nathan would consider. I wouldn't even have expected that of Lex. If not for me, nothing like this might not even be happening today.

The game was really fun. Nobody seemed to want to win just to be able to brag they'd won. All of the children had such pure smiles, so much fun on their face. If any of them thought too much about winning, then they were just spoiling this day for themselves. But, from what I witnessed out on the field, no one seemed that way to me. Well, besides Henry and Nathan. On the bus ride home, I could hear them complaining to one another about the low scores both teams, and they were even worse when they said how their team sucked for having the lower of the two numbers. I was glad the kids were asleep right now. The games we played had tired them out. If they had overheard Henry and Nathan's scathing, insulting words, they might regret ever having had fun, and I would have none of that anymore.

When we stopped back at camp, we tipped the drivers and escorted the children back to their rooms. After that, I had one last thing to do. I went and caught up with Henry and Nathan before they entered their rooms. I put an arm around both of their necks to appear like we were having a friendly chat when I was really using my weight and their momentum to force them forward. We stopped just short of their doors.

"Look, you two can be as pessimistic and standoffish as you want to to me, I could care less," I said. "But don't go out of your way to belittle something these kids have every right to be proud of. I don't want to hear you ever saying what you said on the bus ever again. Are we clear?" I asked. Before they responded, I quickly added. "I'm getting better at the shooting thing. Remember that." I removed my arms from around them and left them there. I didn't have to turn around to know they were nervous. I didn't hear either of their doors open until I was halfway across the yard.

The next year and a half was bit of a breeze for me, honestly. I got to grow up more than I anticipated. I became a sort of older brother for Dende, smoothing things out for him as he continued to expand his horizons. I'd stayed up late night with him, either sitting on the ground to carefully point out the constellations, or test each other with mathematical equations we wrote in the dirt. I would occasionally fill in Amber and Riley on what I'd been up to and we'd laugh and share and share and laugh. Lex and I never split apart as co-teachers, even though we did eventually get a fourth group. Director Michaels had to bring on a fifth member, but was struggling to find one when I had the best idea. I recommended Amber. It took some convincing as she wanted to continue work as a real estate agent, even overseas. I got her to buckle when I mentioned that she'd still have plenty of time to tend to those duties since classes were only two hours a day, and that Lex and I would ease her load by helping her devise lesson plans.

I was forced to await her arrival at the camp as there wouldn't be enough room on the jeep for the driver, Amber, her luggage, and myself. It was nearly 3 pm by the time she arrived, and I wanted her to meet with Lex and Dende, and some of the other students I'd taken a shine too. And they all got along famously.

Amber and Lex were fast friends, which freed up more of my time to continue mentoring Dende. But remember I said that this was part of a long, hard, sad time in my life. Not a happy stretch. The road to this down spiral had begun the moment I saw the news ad and applied for it. And the aftermath, well, it wasn't going to make anyone in this story look good. Unless you remember Steve.

CHAPTER 9

Baboons

There is little joy in the next decade or so of my life. Well, in comparison to the tragedy that wrapped it up. I'm going to do explain based on how my relationships with various people were headed to the crapper. First and most importantly, Amber.

When she first arrived, Amber had loved the life out in Africa we were sharing. It was now a brand new adventure, both for her and for me. To be honest, it didn't seem as much of a chore when she came around. Just like the first day at Neptune Fitness wasn't terrible.

She and Lex were more similar than I had taken the time to notice. Both were full of life, jubilant to be working with jungle children, young enough to be their older sisters. The biggest similarity between those two lovely ladies was that they both enjoyed helping others, which was a given since this was a charitable group. But Amber had a need to help others that was beaten into her by her grandparents. That's why she first reached out to me. She saw a man in need of a little assistance, and she knew how to give it.

The thing was, her thrill of helping me had ended, and so had a strong foundation of our relationship. I wasn't the sick, damaged puppy I was when we met, and it was taking everything she had to stay faithful to us. I figured at the time that it was an issue of my commitment to us, so I proposed. She said yes, and I guess the prospect of being with me through all my ups and downs, particularly the downs, was made her say it.

It had taken about three years of planning and a lot of work, but we were married. Lex was her maid of honor, Dende was my best man. He could be called a man now, actually, just simply for how he looked. He was only 14, but he had muscles, like Riley-sized muscles. And he was tall. His growth spurt was incredible. A six foot tall, reformed club rotund member, but he still looked to me as a mentor, and I was pleased.

Our vows were our own and they were sweet, but I could see the subliminal messages behind hers. Stay fat, stay large, stay broken. I needed you broken. So very broken. I'd need time, years to get you to be what I needed you to be, but I wasn't marching to her tune.

When she could get no satisfaction from trying to mend my "scars", she developed an obsessive need to work the students harder to achieve the level of intelligence that Dende had. She wanted desperately to find a protege to have cling to her advice, her knowledge like I had done. Thing was, I didn't search for it, I stumbled upon it. When that also failed for her, she and I grew hostile toward one another, fighting quiet little battles. Meaningless, childish ones. One day I wouldn't bring her coffee when she slept in. Another, she wouldn't pass me the salt for my mashed potatoes. Things like that. They became our unraveling, but the major tug was yet to be made.

By this point, we were trapped a circle of feigned affection and hidden animosity, but we kept up face. Lex and Dende were still our friends, and they had grown to be friends, too. We wanted them to not have to choose sides for our splitting, so we kept things as amicable as we could.

Lex and I were friends first, but order doesn't necessarily dictate rank. Yes, I was the first to be her friend amongst myself, Amber, and Dende, but Amber was more her type of person to chat with, share secrets with, model herself after. Lex didn't share the same upbringing as Amber. Her desire to want to help people was similar to my own, but she and Amber both had an undying compulsion to fix others' problems. Amber only needed it more. Lex could pick and choose between her options, but she made sure to keep options. In a sense, she and Amber became those for one another without realizing it. I saw they'd reassure one another, the bond evidenced there, but it was fleeting. The more Lex started to grow from that, the more their bond was doomed. Any bond with Amber was doomed, but it seemed that way for me, as well.

Another couple of years had passed by and things had mended between Amber and I somewhat. But now, she had a new issue on her mind. Trying to get back to her original game plan of real estate in Africa. The past five or so years, she'd slowly abandoned that road, but it was here now, and stronger than before. We had started our arguments for a second time, but this one wasn't going to end until we did.

I was content with staying in Africa for the rest of my life, i would repeatedly say to her in hopes it would cease the argument for a couple of days. It would. And I'd enjoy Africa with peace for those same days.

Teaching didn't have the same reward, albeit, since the students were back to being the same old types, year after year. The quiet, studious ones. The loud, rambunctious ones. The bullies. The ones that slacked off just enough to get by. No one stood out. Made an impression. Nobody could differentiate themselves from any predecessor that fell into their group. Dende must have been a lucky break for me. For this village.

Dende has joined the guards when his schooling was deemed over. He was better with a pistol than I was, and had much better survival instincts. I figured that he'd out last all of us, even the students younger than him. I heard the deafening ring that erased all my expectations of his life the same time the entire camp did. We knew instantly what was going down in the brush.

Baboons.

The firing had ended quickly. After the initial panic I felt about the sounds faded away, I was pleased to learn that only about twenty seconds were occupied by the harrowing battle noises. And I thought that was the end of it. It wasn't.

The guards came running into the village with several bodies, each one was drenched with blood from a deadly, fatal gunshot wound. I didn't know three of the boys who's been shot, but the fourth's cobalt blue eyes were trembling, as if urging him to stay alive. Survive a little longer and then you'll be taken care of by the doctors already on scene. That's the look I saw in Dende's eyes as he was dying.

I kneeled down at his die and gripped his hand. His grip was about as tight, which meant there was still life in him. He could make it. He *would* make it. He was a 19 year-old, full of life, packed with muscle and intelligence, wits, and a few good other virtuous traits that I adored about him. The doctors tried desperately to staunch the blood flow from the small, but seemingly gaping wide hole in his chest cavity. I was close to vomiting, but I would've hated myself if any bile had splashed him right now, so I choked it down.

I couldn't believe my eyes right now, even though I had on my glasses. We had just had breakfast this morning, joking about the routine of their sweeps, and how it was always peaceful. The baboons cell had all but vanished. In all my time here, they had never once actually bothered us. I don't know what had changed now, or for whatever reason, but it was not fair to this young man. He had a life to look forward to, a brilliant life. One where he didn't need to face the threat of baboons, or be done in by them.

All it was ever meant to be was a routine sweep of the camp's exterior. That's all. A simple trek through the beautiful scenery the brush provided us those late night we would stare into the starry sky. The brush's midnight glow was something the two of us would keep for ourselves, and it was now just mine. In the blink of an eye, the baboons had raised their venomous tails and struck at Dende's heart. He was gasping for air now, but he turned to me, trying so very hard to pass on a message. I leaned in close to ease his attempt efforts.

"One...true," he gurgled but then regained his breath, "prescription." Those were his final three words. His death was slow, painful, and agonizing to watch, but that was Dende for you. Pushing through until he could solve problems. I'm not sure which one he was referring to now, but he had solved something, and I was going to find out what, but for now, we had four teenage boys dead at our feet, protecting us from a threat we now knew was very real.

If ever there was a time to pack your bags and run, it would be when the young man you saw as a younger brother was gunned down by a splinter cell with an unknown agenda. I couldn't have packed fast enough once the funeral and general grieving over Dende and the other three young men was over. I asked Lex if she was fine with me and Amber up and leaving the fold so suddenly. She said she didn't mind as she would be leaving shortly after us. We learned that she, too, had family in California that she wanted to stay with and told her that she should visit us when she's State-side.

We bade farewell to the jungle children, Henry and Nathan, Director Michaels, and then we headed for our flight home. The next twenty four hours felt like we were in limbo, weightless, like the world wasn't on our heads and shoulders anymore. It was simply, you know, just us. Well, our shells. My body/mind split had occurred, but my mind was recalcitrant when I tried to remember anything about what we may have said to each other on the flight. For all I knew, those were probably the last good words we exchanged.

We got to her place, which she subletted to her sister in exchange that she never use her bedroom. It was pristine when we entered, but a hot mess when we left it. Broken lamps and a smashed remote, a messy, untidy bed, clothes strewn every which way. And that's when the tugging came at our last little bit of a raveled relationship.

We went at each other with no pulled punches. I would call her out on her poor behavior toward me in front of the students, toward her students, and her lack of respect of my dreams. She drove straight in with the rebuttal that I only thought of my dreams, that my devotion was blind, a pathetic attempt to mold our marriage into my own play thing. A toy. When it was used up and old, I would throw it out and find a new one.

To that point, she made ridiculous allegations that Lex and I were engaging in scandalous, salacious activities behind her back. The nerve and the sheer insecurity of that accusation was as painful as being called Porker, and then she brought that up, too.

She said how all of this, me, her, the marriage, Africa, it was all so I could try and reconcile that part of my life. To make it so that it could be rewritten, and she wasn't wrong there. The next part, the part where I was only using people as I see fit to make that happen- that was wrong. The pieces to do that simply fell into my lap at opportune times. I'd not planned on meeting Dende, or even becoming his mentor. His friend. I simply wanted to do something noble. Meeting him was still a part of that, but if I could achieve two goals at once, why shouldn't I?

The last thing she wanted to say that didn't sound like it came from her insecurities was that how I didn't mention her at all when talking about my goals. How she didn't fit in them. She was angry that she had wasted nearly two decades of her life with me, a man that said would never be as devoted to her as she was to me. She said that if I had put sch thought behind my dreams, then surely if I wanted her in my life, she would've been mentioned.

Serving me the divorce papers a year later, that was just her finally making the choice that she was right. And she was. I hadn't given her that time, that same consideration she gave me. I accepted the divorce papers with a smile. It wasn't a whoo-I'm free-of-that-bitch-for-good-smile. It was a I'm-free-to-find-a-new-dream-smile. Except, I had no new dreams, no other aspirations. Africa, for most of this part of my life, was my goal. My endgame. Now, it was just another check point I had passed through. What dream could I come up with? Could one simply just come up with a dream or was it something you just knew one day after a cozy night's rest. I decided that a good night's rest would do me some good. At the very least, it would clear my head and rejuvenate my body.

It felt like I had slept for the next five or six years. I hadn't found any new purpose, and here it was, 2009. I was out of a job, almost homeless. Riley had put me up in his garage. It was nice and spacious, but I wouldn't want to stay here forever. In the final settlements of our divorce, Amber said I could most of my possessions. She said she didn't want or need them, but that I had. She was the college gradu-ate with experience with real estate. I was the college drop-out with an extensive amount of charity work under my belt, but with no real credentials, I wouldn't be accepted as a teacher anywhere in America.

At that moment, sitting in Riley's garage, staring at the turned off television set I'd had since my days with my mother, I gave my life a quick little recap. I lost my best friend. I lost my mother. I lost my younger brother. I lost my wife. And I was only in my late 40s at the time. Ws I going to lose anyone else. Riley? Oh, who am I kidding? If I lost Riley right now, I wouldn't even register it. But the same could not be said for him.

Riley had allowed me access to the main home when I needed to bathe or cook, which wasn't as often as I used to. I didn't have anyone else to freshen up for, or to be well fed for. Diets, exercise, what were they giving me? Headaches and a sour taste in my mouth, that's what.

Riley was out to go and get a haircut. He did the grooming and the bathing and the feeding of himself to appear sane for his dates. He had many. I tried my best not to rain on his parade. He was still young, and in some people's eyes, so was I. He had a life to live, I had one to squander.

I stood in the bathroom and stared into the water I let pool in the sink. In the still reflection, I could clearly make out my facial features. And I didn't like them one bit. I was covered in misshapen, patchy clumps of what I could call a beard. It was gross, filled with remnants of past meals. I think a few pieces of macaroni and cheese, some of that green foliage at the tops of broccoli to make them look like trees.

I took the time to at least clear the leftovers from my beard, but I was not going to attempt shaving. I was already on suicide watch. I had tried to drown myself some weeks ago. Riley had run in and yanked me from the water when he saw water spill beneath the bathroom door, but no shower sounds. Whenever he was gone, all dangerous items and rooms in the house had to be secure. Right now, all the windows were locked, the knives locked away in drawers, and when I turned around, I saw that the tub was covered with a tarp that was duct taped down to the floor. The tarp reached all the way around the tub. If I wanted to drown myself, I'd have to lean over the edge closer to the wall and reach down, but my body was not that long or flexible, so Riley was probably safe as long as he continued that tradition with the tub.

He made the garage livable after that. He removed all the tools, blunt and sharp alike. Screwdrivers, hammers, nails, chains, etc. Nothing I could hang, stab, or bludgeon myself with remained within my vicinity. He allowed me the bare essentials, like a toothbrush, a small, plastic tub he would refill with water every morning and evening before he left for work or a date. He hadn't introduced me to the young lady, but I was glad about that. I didn't need a beautiful woman paraded out before me. It would make me think of Amber, and cause me to have another episode.

What initially made me try to drown myself was the memory of when Riley, her, and I had upgraded our memberships together to be super memberships at Neptune Fitness. Amber and I had just began officially introducing each other to other people as boyfriend and girlfriend. She had encouraged me to remove my shirt and just to float in the water. I did just that and would lay on my back, the cool water rolling relaxing through the grooves of my fat folds. It was better than the massage chairs at the mall. The reason I started to drown was that I fell asleep in that relaxed pose at the gym. Since it worked so well then, I'd try it in a bath tub. More or less, it worked. Riley's tub was too small for me to submerge my entire body, so I had to extend my legs out over the bottom end of the tub and lean my upper body back as far as I could.

Riley made the argument to the doctors that I didn't truly wish to die because when he had stormed in, I had my hands on the edges of the tub and was trying desperately to hold my breath. He said that I had gotten stuck in the tub and that's why he had helped me out. The doctors didn't seem to disbelieve him, but they ordered the suicide watch instructions just to be on the safe side. And there's good reason to, in my opinion.

I was a risk.

The doctors knew it.

Riley knew it.

I knew it.

The days after the suicide attempt were peaceful but long, warm but alone, boring but spent with a friend. I was losing a bit of my mind, pieces that were being swatted away like flies over a picnic table. The flies stopped and retreated to the sound of a phone call, and not to the house phone, to my cell phone. It was a call from Lex.

"Lex tells me that you're an honest, hard worker," said Andre, Lex's brother. He was leading me through the halls of his moving company. It was just wide enough to let me through. There was only one long hallway that stretched from the front to the back where the loading trucks were. Andre ran a moving company called LA Carry and Storage.

"That's correct," I said.

"She also told me that you were cautious, steady, aware of your surroundings."

I knew what he was getting at then and there. "Yes, I'd be a careful mover. I won't drop boxes, break or damage valuables, and be careful of sharp corners and tables along my path."

Andre smiled, pleased. "Good. Now, let me show you the trucks."

He placed an arm around my shoulder like we were old buddies and continued to lead me toward the back lot of the building. I didn't want to get too familiar with him. I'd gained and lost a good number of friends in my life, and losing another was going to break me, I suspected, so I kept my guard up.

And while he was palling around with me, it made me think of Steve. Yes, I'd seen him on television with Wozniak. I wasn't blind to his technological rise through the midst of my turmoil. I knew long ago that he'd won the bet, but at this point, I wasn't sure that I'd keep up my end of the bargain. Yes, at one point, I had a shot, even though at the time, I didn't much think of the bet. All I could see was red.

Andre showed me around the entire office, welcomed me aboard, and then I had a new chance, a chance I didn't see coming. I would still be able to right the wrongs of my child and bare those trials with scars, but the summer had yet to end, and my revelation had not been discovered, but I'll jump straight to that point.

I helped dozens upon dozens of families, all with three trucks or more worth of possessions. I didn't see the change coming because I wasn't looking for it, much in the way that I just happened across Dende the way I did. I had went to my new place that I'd bought about three months into working for Andre. The suicide watch was suspended after a few therapy sessions and a psychologists deemed me mentally fit. Well, enough that I was not at risk of throwing my life away. The therapist mentioned that they would want me to come back for follow up meetings so they could maintain a consistent record of my mental faculties.

In my new apartment, I had showered and noticed- for the first time- that it didn't take as long as usual.

I usually have a good grasp of time, and I knew that I had washed all over, thoroughly as I normally would, but it didn't take as much time to do so. I went out and checked myself in the mirror. The slow changes had crept up on me. My muscles took to the exercise-rules. Come in slowly and surely, and it'll be much easier of an impact when you go all in. Well, muscles couldn't just come all in, they're all gradual. I didn't know it until I had stepped on the scale. It was closing in on the fall of 2009, and I was under 300 lbs, like way under. I was just north of 250 lbs and my arms and legs were looking thinner, leaner, more muscular.

CHAPTER 10

Insurmountable

There I was again, back in the psychologist's office, me on the bench, him in his chair. We were solely on a last name basis because at the time I was, as he described, erecting a wall between my vulnerability and other people, even those I knew prior to the suicide attempt. He was Dr. Harvard and I was Mr. Garbarino. Of course, he knew my first name, but I'd urged him not to say it. No familiarity could be born between us. Not a chance. He was correct about the walls.

"I see you've been losing weight," Dr. Harvard commented.

"That's correct," I answered plainly. I betrayed as little emotion to him as possible. I didn't want him reading into every little expression I made, so each week when I knew I would be coming here, I would spend an hour mentally pasting on my deadpan look. I wanted nothing to be determined by my face. If it didn't come out of my mouth, he was not going to learn about it.

"I must commend you," he said. "I've had plenty of people come in here with that same steel-faced resolve, but none have had the willpower to hold it as long as you. I think the only person that's trumped your time has been a cop."

"Trumped?" I caught the past tense there. Had I slipped up somehow?

"Do not feel discouraged," he said. "Cops have been trained to hold even more broader, scarier expressions. You have nothing to be ashamed over."

I betrayed pride and anger. I narrowed my eyes and leered at Dr. Harvard for just a moment before repasting my deadpan back on, but he'd seen the slip up. If I hadn't done it before, I'd done so this time for certain.

He chuckled lightly. "Works like a charm every single time."

"What are you talking about?" I was curious, but my face didn't display that.

"Like I said, I get people coming to me with such expressions as the one you continue to wear as I speak. I've learned to develop games to make them betray themselves, even they try their very best not to. If I wanted, I could unravel your mask in under five minutes, but that it is not why we're here. We're here to get to the reasons behind your attempt at suicide. What is it you feel you can't solve?"

"Excuse me?" I kept my mask on, regardless of his opinion on the matter.

"When someone quits at anything, it is because of a road block they believe to be insurmountable. What roadblock plagues you?"

What was he talking about? I had no roadblocks. Did I? Dende seemed to think so. His final words seemed to be the answer to a question I hadn't asked him. Did he foresee this or did he just want to give me the answer while he still had the chance? I could feel that if I continued on this train of thought that my mask would be worthless, so I abandoned it for the moment.

"I can honestly say that I do not know what you're referring to," I said in my defense.

"And I believe." He sat forehead, wiggling a pen between his fingertips. "However, we now have something to focus on. Whatever you find to be hampering you is coming undone. You told me in one of our previous sessions that you've had trouble trying to lose weight. I believe the issue was more mental than physical. I don't think you could lose weight because you didn't want to. But right now, something has changed. Your body is finally obeying the orders of your mind and you're losing pounds."

"But that sounds more like a wall was torn down rather than erected." Dr. Harvard was confusing me.

"Not torn down. Renovated. The blockage is just focused on another aspect of your life now. I believe it and the wall you've made are related."

"Are you positive about that?"

"Not positive enough. I want you to reflect on our conversation we just had and think of what it spells for your life. There must be something you can think of that could be the cause."

I nodded. "I'll get right on that, Dr. Harvard."

I wouldn't, but that was because I didn't know where to start. How could I analyze myself. Subjective analyses could be riddled with inaccuracies. I could simply change a few adjectives around while relaying the message to make myself sound better. I'd ask Riley, but our relationship had served its purpose in my eyes. I needed a place to stay, he was a person I could ask for such a favor. I asked, I stayed, I moved on. If he reached out to me, I would answer, but me going to him, that wasn't going to happen anymore.

I was a little late for dinner, but I think that Lex and Andre would understand. The two of them were as close as friends as I wanted right now. I was familiar with them, but not so close that it would cripple me to lose them like it was with my mother and Amber and Dende. My mother caused me to be emotionally crippled long term, but I was so shaken that I couldn't move for the rest of that day. Amber's leaving me was a long expected journey, so it left me only minorly physically crippled. I had very few physical spaces to turn to, so I was prone in a shelter-my-way sense. Dende's passing had left me so drained that it was a miracle I had strength to even argue with any of Amber's long rants about devotion and compromise.

Lex had prepared one my favorite dishes of hers, grilled chicken marinated in lemon juice, garnished with basil and diced mushrooms, a side of peppered corn, and lemonade. I know I said that lemons were the most heinous of all fruits, but the citrus flavoring seemed to complement the chicken very well. The tanginess of the mushrooms, in their tiny proportions, balanced the flavor out nicely. The peppered corn was just fantastic by itself, with or without the chicken. And lemonade, well, who could hate lemonade, byproduct of the dastardly fruit or not.

"So, Lex, how goes it at the daycare?" I asked. I was still keeping my wall strong, but for a social gathering such as this, a different mask was required, one where i looked like I was having a good time. I mean, I was, favorite dish and all before me, but the mask made it seem less real and better for me in the long run.

"It's going pretty good. We're getting more and more families bringing their children to our doors, so business has steadily been improving." Lex had struggled about as much as I did to find a job when she came back to America. She decided that if she couldn't find a job, why not start one for herself? She found a few other people on Craigslist in need of employment, and together, the three women made their own daycare facility called Sun Valley Sitters. The main service is to house and entertain children of clients, but Lex then thought of adding a sideline service of loaning out temp babysitters to families more active at night. "One of our babysitters, Laney, she just got a job as a steady babysitter for this wealthy family out in Burbank."

"That's amazing," I said, but I didn't care. I was careful not to say that out loud.

"But enough about me," she said. "How're things going for you guys at the moving company?"

"I get by," I said, hoping to keep things modest. Andre had other plans.

"Are you kidding me? 'Get by.'" He turned to his sister-in-law. "This guy puts on the muscles and shreds the pounds like taking breaths. One day he came in and I thought we had hired someone new without my approval. I mean, look at him." He faced me again. "Jack, stand up."

I did.

"Look at those arms. They're getting closer to being bigger than mine. And his legs," he whistled, "It's like he was being slowly replaced, piece by piece, exchanging parts of his soul in return."

Lex giggled. "You didn't make a deal with the devil, now, did you, Jack?"

I had to laugh myself. I rolled up my sleeves and prepared to enjoy the meal when Lex looked stunned for a moment, staring at my bicep. "What's wrong?"

"Is your arm bleeding?" she asked, her voice shaky from being alarmed.

I looked at what she was referring to and understood her confusion. "Oh, no. This is a tattoo."

Andre raised his eyebrows. "Since when did you get a tattoo?"

"I got it about maybe two weeks ago." I rolled up my sleeve all the way and showed it to them. It was a dark line with a red mane, encircled by a red square. There were some clouds fluttering about the lion, too.

"Why a lion?" Lex asked.

"Oh, my middle school's mascot was a lion. I'm starting to have the body that I wished I had back then, so I figured it was a good way to symbolize my change, even though many years have passed since."

"I think it's a cool idea," Andre remarked. "I have scars from my middle school years from jumping fences and raiding junk yards for scraps of metal to build my own bikes. I remember those times fondly whenever I see one of the scars in the mirror."

"I wish my memories were positive. While I do have pride in what I've been going through, the memories of where I started at were a pain in my ass. I wish I could forget them, but roots are roots, and they stick with you, no matter how badly you wish you could...block them...off..."

Lex and Andre gave me confused looks when I suddenly trailed, off, but I believe I was having a breakthrough, or an epiphany about what Dr. Harvard and I were discussing earlier. He said that there was a new roadblock somewhere that allowed my body to begin dropping the pounds, and it could be linked to my childhood. That was the biggest thing I shared in common with Dende, so he'd be able to know if it still affected me or not, since I'm sure it affected him, even when he died at my feet.

I politely excused myself from the table to make a quick call to Dr. Harvard. I'd asked him if he could squeeze me in tomorrow or the next day for a session. He said tomorrow was no good, but the day after he could pencil me in for a session lasting from 3:30-4:30 pm. I agreed to the time and we terminated the call.

I returned to the dinner table and Lex, Andre, and I continued to discuss my tattoos. I told them that I was thinking of a second one, but had no idea what it would be, or for that case, *where* it would be. Lex said that as long as it didn't make her panic if she only caught a glimpse of it, she was fine with the choice. Andre sort of gave a cheer and then we banged our glasses together. I was glad I had that approval, but part of me wanted that approval seeking phase to be over. I sought it from so many people and yet no one wanted it from me.

I spent all of the next day biding my time, thinking of what Dr. Harvard might actually discuss about my breakthrough, or what questions I could bring up to better help me understand my situation. Nothing seemed to spring out before me, so I guess playing it by ear was going to be my play. I'd have to make sure to plaster on my dead-pan mask before the session. I needed a much better one this time, more impenetrable than before.

"Hey, Dr. Harvard," I said when I rolled into the office. His assistant shut the door behind me. I sat down on the couch, refusing to lay down right away.

"Hi, Mr. Garbarino. How are you doing?" he asked so plainly that it almost startled me. I looked into his face and caught on to what he was doing. He was imitating my deadpan face perfectly, to a tee.

I shut my eyes slowly and inhaled that way, too. I needed to absorb my surprise at a snails pace to avoid betraying shock. "I'm doing fine. And yourself?"

"Why did you request that we meet again this week?" He turned and leered directly into my eyes that were so still that he'd clearly done this before. They were like the best of predators, waiting as frozen in place as stones, waiting for the most opportune time to strike.

"I believe I've stumbled across the...roadblock, as you described it."

"And what makes you so certain that you did? Are you positive?"

"I'm not certain I did. And I'm not positive about anything," I said with the same cold detachment he was tossing my way.

"Very well, then. Well, tell me what you've learned. I'm all ears."

"It goes back to my roots. I believe that my previous roadblock was linked to my childhood and that's why I couldn't lose weight. For some reason, I probably didn't want to. But now, I can. However, it seems that now it's targeting me through my memories. I think I've been trying to section them off unconsciously. While trying to deny myself access to the bad ones, I'm locking them all away."

"That's an interesting theory. And does that bother you?" This time, he was the one who slipped up, but he made no move to correct his error. He stayed leaned forward, keenly intrigued by my case.

"To be honest, more than I thought," I admitted. "As much as I despise the things that happened to me, they did all shape me to the man that I am now, the man I've always been up to this point."

"And what man would that be?"

That question was yet to be answered. We went back and forth discussing that, but nothing we mentioned seemed to hit on what I was becoming now.

That was my last time going to see Dr. Harvard. I appreciated his help, but I didn't need a psychologist any longer to tell me if I was going to go off the rails again. I knew I wouldn't. I had something about myself to discover, and I was on the verge of making a massive decision. It was two years away from its earliest conception, but I knew now that I wasn't going to run from anything. In fact, I was doing the opposite. I was running to what made me attempt to kill myself so I could confront it, challenge it, and overcome it.

CHAPTER 11

My new team

In the two years since quitting my sessions with Dr. Harvard, I had fully thrown myself into the moving job. I was healthy, for the argu- ably the first time in my life. Like, long term healthy and not just those short periods of time sucking down terrible diet food and spending a ludacris amont of hours at Neptune Fitness. I was feeling less and less need for my mask, I was looking and feeling better than I cold recall ever being able to do, and I had friends. Lex and Andre. I wasn't plan- ning to lose them, not if I could help it.

There was one day when Andre had asked me what my secret was. What I was doing to shed nearly 150 lbs in just two years? I didn't have the answer then because I wasn't sure myself. But now, I was (sure that I had the answer). I researched it day and night, well, every night. During every waking hour of my days, I was doing what helped me shed the unneccesary girth. During the few hours at night I had to myself, I spent my time researching exactly why every part of my body seemed to love this new, for lack of a better word, workout.

I mean, moving people every single day was not easy, certainly more of a hassle than any gym. When you're on the move, like on your feet, it grants more allowance for tension to build in one's muscles. From your legs up, weight shifts with every step. Each time your raise and lower a foot to the ground, the tension is spread to every fiber, ev- ery tendon, every ligament you own. At the gym, your body is station- ary, absorbing all the tension in specific, localized areas like your arms and chest. But working out this way, *my* way, was much better.

There are a few examples that can be drawn from simple tasks that everyone who moves from home to home would know about, but just not the full potential behind it. Simply lifting boxes of materials, the repetitiveness of that activity, it's the basics of one my new workour staples. Marching back and forth with 20-35 lb boxes while in motion does work a good number of muscles, from your arms, back, chest, and your calves. Standing erect and using your legs to support more of the weight just increases tghe amount of muscles that can be built up in your lower body. Leaning back as you walk is a negative. Putting all that weight on your back is dangerous. Pooling such tension at the base of your spine could lead to paralysis, at least based of what I can understand of the six simple machines.

If you have a lever and try to open a metal door with it with all your weight, it would either snap the lever, which would either be a metal rod of some sort, maybe a crowbar. That would happen to someone's spine if they put too much pressure on it by lifting more than they're capable of too often and for an extended period each time.

I'd actually come to make a game out of that particular exercise that Andre and I would play when he'd force me to take a couple of days off, only to make sure I avoided overdoing things. We hadn't given the game a name yet, but if you've heard of Speed Stacking, then you'll understand the dynamic much easier.

Speed Stacking is a game where being dextrous over strong counts. It involves the stacking and unstacking of cups in specific formations. The standard is twelve cups, but you can do it with more if you've trained enough. There are five main formations for the standard twelve-cup set. One-ten-one. Three-six-three. Six-Six. Three-three-three-three. Twelve. The twelve is the same as the one-ten-one, but the two cups on the sides are stacked right up against the ten while the one-ten-one leaves a fair amount of space between the ones and ten stacks.

The game Andre and I invented isn't as complicated as that. We both stand at the ready, a stack of boxes at our sides. The goal of the game is to move the boxes from one stack to another and then back again. The first one to deconstruct and then reconstruct the original stack is the winner. We were even in our win-loss ratios.

Another of the exercises that I'd come to love that Andre wold share with me, and this one we dubbed the "Couch Relay", involved- you guessed it- couches. We would both grab hold of one end of one the spare couches we purchased just for this purpose. We would grab and raise the couch and run from one end of his backyard to the other. Each time we made it back to his back door, we would squat a little lower and do it again. When we first started this workout, we could only bend down so far that Lex was able to stand by us at eye level. Now, we were able to squat down to her waist and run from one end of the yard to his back door. Actually, with our lowered positions, it looked more like were scuttling little crabs. Moving sideways with our legs bent out at our sides.

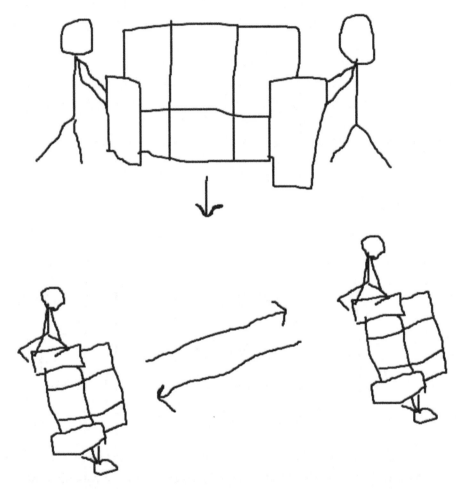

We're thinking of giving it a new name. Andre's desperate to call it the "Crab Couch Race", but I thought we should leave the word crab out of it. Regardless of the name, the exercise would be a brilliant conditioner for those who run for a living. Soccer players could strengthen their legs at an incredibly fast rate. The tendons in their calves and shins would become a fortified mass of iron. If they couldn't before, they'd be able to split soccer balls with one powerful blow. The sound of the soccer ball popping would pale in comparison to the demonstration of pure muscle capacity.

Runners, kickboxers, and swimmers could all do with stronger legs to propel themselves and strike harder than ever. I'm sure they had their own regimens that licensed coaches were strictly adhering them to, but it didn't mean my invention wouldn't be even a little helpful.

While each of my workouts did target every muscle in the human anatomy, unless my night time research was failing me, each of my workouts do indeed target specific areas of the body more than others. The boxes have the arms and back, the couches have the legs and arms, and the chairs have the chest and arms. Oh, we haven't gone over chairs yet. Well, no time like the present.

CHairs were more versatile in regards to the kinds of workouts Andre and I had concocted together. Well, I came up with them, and he would try to think of names, but so far, only my end seemed to be productive. A good way to think of it would be to say that chairs were the free weights of my style of exercise.

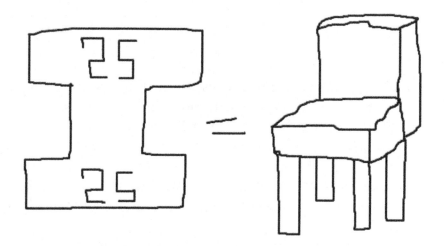

One of the first exercises that Amber had showed me was one of the main ones that I used chairs for. I would riase them to my waist and hold them there for a second, raise the chari above, lower it to my shoulders, and then back down to my waist. The thing that made this better than an actual free weight was based off of the age old adage: bigger is better. Since the chair had a better and more defined distribution of weight within in, it made for a better tool for physical exertion. Simply holding it at my wiast, even without moving around, put more stress on my entire arm, not just my forearms.v

Doing squats with them over your head was a way to center the heat in your abdomen, squeezing it there, trapping it with the pressure of clench, tight abs. As you slowly rose from the squatted position, the heat would explode from the relief and rush through all the neighboring muscles, looking for a safe shelter to reside in. It had many options and suitors. The heat would invite itself to your thighs, chest, and back.

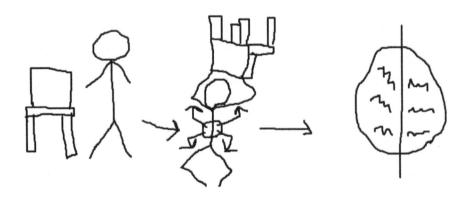

It took me some time to realize just what Andre was trying to do, but to me, this was just something I enjoyed doing. I wasn't hoping to do anything more than live out the rest of my life with him and Lex and a good bill of health- at long last. It was Tuesday, and Andre had urged me into one of my forced off days. Lex was off at her own job, so I was alone when I turned the tv on. I'm glad I was, because seeing what I saw on the news's headlines shook me more than I thought it ever would.

The headline read "Apple CEO, Steve Jobs, Has Passed Away".

I tuned it out after they said the words "due to pancreatic cancer". A health issue. Of all things, my childhood friend, who, by any and all means, was healthier than I was, died of an illness. I couldn't comprehend the meaning of that irony. I had almost died because of health when he, around that same time, dropped out of college to pursue his own goals. I didn't know he had dropped out at the time, but when he became the face of Apple, his life became an open book for anyone with a computer. And here he was, at the pinnacle of his career, and all of the sudden (to me, at least), he was gone. I tried many different ways of rationalizing the situation.

OK, Steve Jobs was sometimes a proud kid, maybe he only got more prideful as he grew up. He certainly had the right to be proud with a nice family, a wife and kids, and a multi-million dollar company that he started. I was as close as I going to get to those years ago. But, right when he had so much to continue living for, to continue progressing and learning, whether it was as a father, husband, entrepreneur. It didn't seem fair. And this, just like with my father, felt wrong. When a man had so much to live for, was that when he was meant to be taken from this world? Would a God, if there was indeed one out there, allow such wrongdoings to transpire? And not even just the God my father worshipped. Maybe other Gods out there were just as at fault for the deaths of great men. I was starting to think they only spared the weaker ones, the ones that they could find even more entertainment from. Perhaps that's why I was able to live when men and women, like Steve Jobs, my father and mother, and Dende had to lose theirs. I didn't like it one bit.

Another possibility that crept up on my mind was something I hadn't been able to recall until I found myself reciting "Stevey" out loud, over and over. I was fooled to think of that version of him as they paraded a photo of him smiling the same way he did when I christened him with that nickname. It reminded me of Petey, the museum, and the gladiator statue. Petey told me that the gladiators were merely playthings for- what did he call them?- hedonistic something-or-others that took pleasure in watching the soldiers battle one another to the death. Wss that what we were doing on this Earth? Battling one another, in one way or form, to the death? Or were we all racing to death faster?

If so, in my scope of the board, I was starting to fall in last place. My father hit a homerun with his quick leave of us. Net came my mother, although she was tagged out. Dende was trying to steal second when the glove caught him on his right breast. Steve Jobs, I couldn't even think of a suitable analogy for him. It didn't seem like his death fit the board. It seemed wrong, a blasphemy, as if the rules suddenly changed. Yes, Steve was part of my world at one point, but as far as any overseeing, all-knowing God, or hedonist asshole knew, we were as far as done with each other as two people could be. Well, other than Amber and I, but I was hoping that thought stayed solely inside my head. As bad as a falling as we had, I didn't want her to become the next target for some deity's drunken amusement.

I cut the television off. I was in no mood to continue watching. I'd be caught up in even more reminiscing than I wanted to. But soon I learned that it was too late, I already was.

I couldn't help when I tried to change clothes. I caught a glimpse of the lion tattoo on my right arm. From there, I stripped down to my pants. The lion was my middle school's mascot, the same beast that Harrison wore a symbol of. Unless he had gotten the ink of a lion sewn into his skin, I was the more devoted of us to the beast's power, the strength it held. I remember when I first considered getting it. At that moment, I was thinking of Steve. So, perhaps, he was somehow loosely tied into my world. Both versions. Steve Jobs and Stevey.

When I walked into the tattoo parlor, I could feel the ghost of Steve tugging at me, trying to persuade me against my decision. This was the bet all over again. I was taking on the lion's disciple the first time, but the second, I was letting the lion purchase on my body. And there I was in my bedroom, staring at that same mark, the insignia.

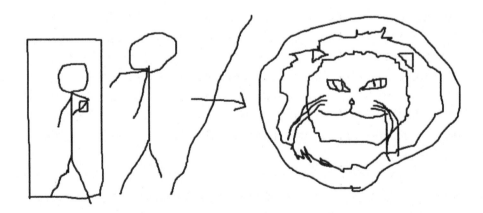

Perhaps that is why I never once encountered a lion in all of my stay in Africa. The mark served as a ward, a barrier, between the predator and myself, and thankfully, those around me. And maybe that's why the deity that learned of my blithe defiance to danger chose to strike with baboons instead.

I was crying and I knew it the moment I heard the plop of water droplets against my wooden floor. I wasn't sad, I was furious. I had a foe, in some form, out in the world, in the wind, and I couldn't combat their decisions no matter how hard I tried. I was but a speck of dust in their eyes, or whatever they used to gaze down upon this world.

How was I to defeat them? Assuming such a feat was possible. How could I make sure to keep entertaining them? Could I be spared then? Would I be? Were they watching me now? Choosing the right time? Waiting for me to wrap the noose round my neck so they could deliver the push? The fear of the possibilities cooking up in my head were so intense that it forced my body/mind split.

I was floating there, in my living room, watching my body attempting to do the math of things that have transpired in the wake of my choices. Choices regarding friends, loved ones, family. I couldn't do the math without the variables present. I needed the variables present. The next move I made was to my computer, an Apple MacIntosh product (maybe this was my connection to Steve since I bought it to celebrate his success). I did a quick (long) internet search.

Twenty-four hours was a long trip. The first time, I'd been pumped to start a dream I had long since developed. Currently, I was dreading touching down on this soil for a second time. The end results of my dream were buried here. All remnants of my time in Africa either slowly faded from my conscience, locked in a box in the darkest, ugliest place of my soul. The only things that still existed outside of that box for me was Lex. But right now, I'd needed to unlock that box and unleash one of my innermost demons. I needed to have a chat with Dende.

It seemed that things for A Can for Africa, A Can for Everyone, was doing much better these days. The main office that used to be a flimsy tent with large, white drape over it was now a solid building, pristine on the outside with polished walls and windows, two intricately carved wooden doors, and a tiled roof. The inside was just as impressive. There were a few cubicle spaces to my right with diligent workers at their stations filing, reporting, documenting, etc. There was a slim hallway that went straight through to the back. At the end of the hall was one door. The plaque on the front of it read "Office of ACAACE Director, Florence Michaels".

I stepped inside and there sat Director Michaels. He'd aged extremely well, still looking young enough to be considered a peer of myself. He looked up at me and I saw the impressive gears in his head accelerate when he spotted me.

"Mr. Garbarino?" he asked. His voice was the only physical feature of his that seemed to had changed since we last saw each other. It was softer now, as if age was eating away at his voice box. Outside may have appeared intact, but his interior was probably suffering as scheduled.

"Yep, that's me," I replied. I was conflicted. Would I wear my mask for him or not. He knew me before the mask existed, so I kept it off. "How've you been?"

"Well, I'm still kicking, same as this place. So, I can't complain."

"I'm happy to see it's still running myself." It meant not everything had ended here with Dende. Director Michaels was quite shaken by the news, to such an extent that rumors circled the camp grounds that he was thinking of pulling the plug on the entire thing.

"Are you here to volunteer again?" he asked with an edge to his voice. "I wouldn't want you to feel like you need to." And there was the reason why. He'd pitied me. And I couldn't blame him. I didn't stick around very long after Dende's funeral. Three days after, I was a ghost in the camp if people still expected to see me return.

"No," I said. "I'm here to see Dende's grave. Would you happen to know where it was moved?"

Director Mich- Florence, as he insisted I call him now that we were not in a professional relationship, joined myself and a driver to the cemetery where they'd moved Dende to. We initially buried him in Mossel Bay, but when his family got wind of what happened, they wanted him buried with them- not with their bodies, they weren't ghosts- but with them in their town. They had their own natural burial ground. Direc- Florence was more than willing to make their wish come true and we moved him to his hometown of Dysselsdorp.

We got there in less than six hours of travel, most of which Florence had stayed asleep. His muscles- also internal- and energy seemed to be reflecting his age more, too. With him asleep, the conversation dropped to nothing. The driver kept his eyes peered on the road and I was keeping vigil on the brush to the left and right of our jeep. I saw butterflies, birds, and monkeys- no baboons.

We made it to Dysselsdorp, a place I couldn't pronounce, so Florence did all the speaking when we arrived. He went in and found Dende's parents, Akhando and Druscille. They were both around Florence's age, but only Druscille looked it. Akhando was younger than he should. I looked into those deeply shining cobalt blue eyes and it was like looking at Dende all over again. I shuddered.

"Are you Jack?" Akhando asked, like he was referring to some higher official, his hands trembling with a pointed finger.

"Yeah, that's-"

Florence nudged my side and then whispered in my ear. "I told these people whta you did for your son and they have come to revere you as a greater man than you might think yourself. Do not shatter their conceptions."

I nodded.

"Yes, sir. I am Jack."

I turned to Florence and he gave a slight nod. I assumed the better I spoke to his parents, the more likely that they wouldn't be broken or disappointed.

"Thank you for watching over our son," Akhando said.

"It was my pleasure, sir. I would've have taken that bullet if I'd been with him at the time. I can promise you that."

"We don't want your promises, Jack," Druscille spoke up.

"Then what is it that you wish of me?" I sounded pretentious, but it's what they wanted.

"We want to thank you. You did save our son, Jack. He wrote back one day, years before he died. The only thing he wrote of was you."

"When he would write home before then, all he would speak of us wanting to come home," Akhando added.

"You saved our son from a lonely death." And with tears in her eyes that only a mother could shed, she embraced me. Her grip was surprisingly tight for as aged as she looked. I guess she and Florence were polar opposites. She was older on the outside, him on the inside. Akhando, I was sure he'd be young on both counts.

They lead me to Dende's grave and he was buried in a row by himself. All the other graves were neatly placed in uniform rows, but his was off in its own little corner. His headstone read the same as it did back at his funeral. "Here lies Dende. Outstanding student, devoted guardian, an honored son and friend. R.I.P."

I turned to his parents and Florence. "I'd like a few minutes alone with him, if you'd please." They all awarded me that and made themselves scarce. When I turned back to his headstone, I envisioned the first version of Dende I'd seen. It morphed from that to his oldest, final version in a few seconds. I envisioned him with a smile. He died with one, he'd have one now if he were standing before.

"How you been, Dende?" I asked the specter.

No real response, but I pictured him saying "I'm doing good, Mr. Garbarino. How about you?"

"As you can see, I'm in better shape, so I'm doing fine. What do you think about it?"

There was no actual response, but true to his character, I had to make him answer regardless. "I think you're fooling yourself. You're not happy."

I was confused now. "What do you mean?"

"You've forgotten your dream," the specter said to me.

"I achieved my dream. I came out here to help kids like you. I did it. I'm good."

He was silent. Right, I had to ask him a question.

"Why do you think I've forgotten my dream?"

"Because you stopped helping us."

"I stopped because I was done. I wanted a new dream. What's wrong with that?"

"Dreams aren't like work assignments, Mr. Garbarino. You can't just pluck one from a bulletin board and say "Ooh, this dream should work nicely.""

"So, what, I can only have one dream per life?"

The specter was gone. I had nothing else to say to someone that didn't wish to listen, so, I too, left.

That trip was not worth it in the end. I'd learned nothing. I'd gotten no closer in my goal to learn why things were happening the way they were around me. Dende said that I still had a dream to follow through on, but my dream was over and done with. Wasn't it?

The first time the hedonists tried to remove me from this world, I had just dropped out of college, reeling from my mother's passing.

What had stopped them? I met Amber, I started the diet, I went to the gym. Were they mocking my truest attempts to stay alive after they had spared me? I would laugh at someone who did just the opposite. The person who ruined their life after being given a second chance was the joke. I was an inspiration…

Dende had mentioned that I wasn't done helping people, being their rock, their coach, their role model. Was that why I was alive now? Because I still had a purpose? It seemed legitimate to think so, but Dende was much younger than me. I'm sure he still had a purpose, or would've had one if only he'd just been grazed by that damned bullet.

I didn't think of the grim intricacies of what Dende's role was in the grand scheme of things too much because the only conclusion that I could reach was that he was simply to be my jumping off point. I didn't want to believe it, but here he was again, as a ghost, and he had set me on that path once more. I was going to do something meant to help others, and not just children, grown ups, people in all phases of their life.

I still had seven hours left in my flight back to California and I was in no rush to get to sleep. And I wanted to, I wouldn't be able to. I had to think of the deaths of all my other important people. My parents, I could only take those at face value without tearing up again. They were my parents, they were older, and it was natural for a child to outlive their folks.

Steve, however, his death was a trigger for me, too, but I had to gamble there was more behind that. Steve was a successful man, one who employed many and I'm sure they all had reasons, either just one or one thousand, to love and/or respect him. Even after he abandoned me when we were children, I could sound off ten reasons to respect him this very instant. He was my friend. He was nice. He was driven. He was compassionate. He was brilliant. He was a good father. He was a loyal husband. He was talented. He was Stevey. He was Steve.

He'd built up his company, his reputation, and all from a single idea. He developed it, promoted it, designed it, expanded it, shared it. I could understand now why he could pass on. His dream was going to be able to go on beyond his life, and that was nothing to sneeze. Leaving behind an empire. It's something only the truest of visionaries could hope to achieve. I wasn't a visionary, but I wanted my mark on this world to expand beyond my life span.

I was in my 50s. My life was already half over. I had no illusions I would make it to see 100. If I did, then the hedonists were simply just a bunch of assholes who truly applied no order to the things they did. If I had to guess, I'd give myself a good, twenty-five, maybe thirty more years before I bit the dust. I was going to do something incredible before then. First, I had to talk to Andre. Whatever he was thinking, I knew I'd want to give it a shot. I had no ideas of my own, so at the very least, his proposal could inspire me.

No, I had another stop to make first. I wanted to know that the hedonists could try and own my all they wanted, but I was not bending a knee. I was going to throw a spear. And that's I stuck on my right breast. I went to the same tattoo parlor and got my second set of ink. It was of a gladiator standing on the edge of a mountain, the implication was that the mountain pierced the heavens and that I was facing the hedonists deities with a long spear in my hand. I had on the helmet with red fluff on top, the gilded armor, the open-toed boots, and a red cape. It was plastered permanently right above my heart. My heart was in this to combat the fiends that dared to control my world the way the did.

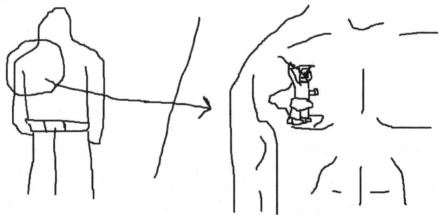

I wanted to be authentic and knew that my full head of hair would not permit me to wear such a helmet, so I went to the barber next and had my head shaved clean, my beard trimmed down until it was a neat, well groomed mustache/goatee combination.

I went home immediately after. I hadn't allowed myself to rest since

getting off of the plane. I was hungry, but in no mood to cook anything, so i went straight to my bedroom and fell asleep as quickly
as I could. I knew now that Dende, as always, with his infallible wit
and wisdom, was right. I hadn't been following my dreams, I'd been
neglecting them. But this time, the dream came roaring with a vengeance.

I was in the living room of my current apartment and was fully
dressed. I was dressed for a marathon. I had on a red muscle shirt,
dark sweatpants with a grey streak down the middle of the pants legs.
The room was empty otherwise.

I was startled by a sudden flash of light, the flashes that cameras
give off, and it was followed by the click of the image capture, but I'm
afraid all it snapped a portrait of was me shielding my eyes from the
flash. Now, I stood in a street. It wasn't empty, but cars weren't what
traversed it, but a marathon of faceless people. They all had on the
same outfit as I did. Who were these faceless people? Where were the
cameras that took photos? That last question was targeted to the cameras that took the previous series of photos and to the ones that were
snapping them now.

After this series of flashes, I was now dressed in a nice suit, standing
before a crowd of people. They, too, were faceless. In the very back was
a cluster of smaller people. I could just barely make out their darker
complexions against the darkness. The jungle children were here?

I didn't know what was happening, but I looked down at my cue
cards. I subtly shuffled through them , but they each contained the
same message written across them in perfect cursive. They all read:
"Read."

I disregarded them and searched the audience. Without faces to
react to, I had no clue if what I said next would be taken well or not, or
if I should use those cues to change the tone of my voice or adjust my
body language. I couldn't make them wait any longer.

"Hi, my name is-"

I don't know what I was expecting, but I was blindsided by a third
set of camera flashes. When my vision corrected itself, I was smiling. I
couldn't help it. Whatever my dream was doing it had hit its mark this
time. I was standing before a wide, jumbo screen tv. It was just hover-
ing right in front of me, like this world only consisted of it and myself.

I was able to stand- or float- there and watch some of my happiest memories pass before my eyes. They went by in no particular order, chronological or otherwise, but they were all happy. Whether the happiness was fleeting or if it ended badly, this screen caught the moment that happiness slashed at my cheeks with a smile.

I saw the time I had lost my first tooth and had awoken to find a dollar underneath my bed.

The next one one after that was the day I'd met Steve Jobs. It was in passing in the halls. One of the meaner children had pushed me and I dropped my milk. Thankfully it was still closed. Steve picked it up and handed it to me. I missed the next few because the tears streaming from my eyes needed to be wiped, and they were persistent little pests.

The third memory I had seen was the ending to my first date with Amber. We had went to a movie and dinner. Lame?- yes. Fun?- yes. Kiss at the end?- yes.

The fourth and fifth were memories that involved my father and church. I'd forgotten all about those since church was a taboo place and subject for me and my mother for most of my life. The first of the two memories was my father taking a picture with me, us in matching suits. The second was of me watching him console our pastor who'd received news of one of his family members passing in mid-sermon.

Lots more passed, ones I'd forgotten because of the stress of the end results. There were times when Dende and I would return the spotted tarantulas to the brush together. Another time was when Amber and I were fighting constantly. Not a happy moment, I know, but we also had angry sex, too. I guess shallow happiness still counted.

I didn't know why I was seeing all of those times then. Was I dying? I wasn't sure. Now that I had everything to lose, would those bastards in the unfair heavens rip me from this world? Was my life flashing before my eyes? It seemed like a far away idea in my mind. Dying? I had no time for it.

I turned away from the screen and looked into a large, black expanse. Nothing existed there, not even the light coming off of the screen behind me. It was a void, and I felt if I stepped forward, I would be lost. But if I turned around, I would be lost anyway.

I turned to my chest and removed my shirt. I stared hard at the gladiator tattoo inked on my skin. I said that I was not going to cow to the heavenly powers that be. I wouldn't. Won't. I clenched my fist tight, gritted my teeth, and leered into the void. I raised my fist and gave a deadly warning. "My true prescription...it's..." I trailed off because my voice had choked off, but I knew what I wanted to say.

And it wasn't just that one word that was being choked off. I found it increasingly hard to breathe. I was gasping for air in a vacuum. No air, no oxygen. I was dying. I felt the darkness closing in around me. I turned and faced the screen. It was losing brightness, the settings bar for it lowering to the lowest grade of brightness it had. Then, it vanished into the void.

I smiled.

I was not going to die in my dream and leave a look of fear on my real world face. If Andre or Lex came in and found my body, I wanted them to know I died happy. If the screen had stayed, right now, this moment would be playing on it. My last moment would be my last sight. I would be fine with that.

The darkness snatched me and swallowed me whole.

I woke with a long, and I mean *long*, inhalation. I gripped my throat and felt the warmth of my Adam's apple. I touched myself all over, and everything was warm. I was alive, but still surrounded by darkness. I climbed out of bed and raced to the lamp near my bedroom door. I turned it on and the blaze of light was searing as I kept my opens wide open, but I was happy to see I was in a familiar place again. I wasn't being tortured by things I couldn't see or hear. I snapped my fingers to test the latter. My ears worked just fine.

I just stood stationary for a time, stunned. I didn't make a move, wouldn't, not until I was positive I wasn't dreaming anymore. I was fine with having dreams, as n goals, but having dreams while I slept. I couldn't take that anymore. I sure hope they had pills that could restrain one's subconscious from running amuck, but if they did, I'm sure they would become America's next top drug.

It had been almost an hour when I finally wiggled my toes. I inched closer and closer to my bed when I finally decided the dream was over. I could go to bed. However, sleeping in it, that wasn't happening by choice. If I fall asleep tonight, it was going to be my sheer loss of the fight to stay awake, not by choice.

I woke up the next morning, dangerously close to the afternoon, and got dressed quickly. I found my cell phone and had four missed calls and a text message from Andre. I unlocked my phone and terminated the missed calls. The message said "I know you're just getting back from Africa, so you don't have to come in today. However, I need you to make sure you make up today on the weekend." And that was doable.

I had a quick breakfast and got ready to spend my day reflecting on Dende's last words to me. The specter Dende, not the real Dende.

He said "You've forgotten your dream."

I knew what dream he meant the moment he said that, but I wanted to fight against it, to declare that I'd wanted a new point to my life. The specter argued and said dreams can't be manufactured. But if not, how does one determine their dream? When I founded my dream of helping people, it was simply so I could do something honorable with my mother's life insurance. I hadn't thought I'd made a life commitment.

Well, I hadn't back then. Now, with this fresh tattoo, which was still covered for the time being while the skin settled, I all but said I would devote my entire being to a just cause. A cause to help those like Dende. I was the gladiator, one of the people who entertain, who tickle the spirits of higher forces. That's what I was now. What I was before, it filled me with unbearable guilt and dread.

I was happy when I met with Lex and Andre for dinner. I didn't need to be alone with my thoughts right now. Company was the enemy of insanity.

"He remembered you? After all these years?" Lex asked, referring to Florence.

"Yeah, it shocked me, too," I said. "Though if I showed up now, he may have to blink to adjust to the change." I rubbed my bare scalp.

"I don't blame him," Andre said. "The cueball look fits you, but it certainly makes you look like a different person."

"That was sort of the point." I rubbed my head once more and then lowered both hands to my lap. "I was being worshipped by Dende's parents, and as much as that showed me the true depth of their respect for me, it felt...like too much. I wasn't this saint they saw me for. I felt bad pretending to be one, but Florence assured me they needed it more than the real me."

"But it was the real you," Lex stated.

"The actions were me, yes, but not the man they thought was behind them."

"Well, then use this transformation of yours to be the man they saw you to be," Andre commented.

That was a thought. Speaking of thoughts. "Andre, you've been working on something lately. Jotting down notes every time we exercise together, before and after. Mind telling me what you've been cooking up?"

He and Lex turned to each other and exchanged cheeky smiles. She would be in on it. Brother and sister, these two didn't hide much from another, if anything.

"I'll be right back." Andre excused himself from the dinner table and jogged inside of his house.

I leaned over closer to Lex. "Any hints as to what I should be expecting?"

"A good laugh," Lex said. That was all the information I needed. Lex and Andre may share everything, but Lex and I understand everything about each other.

Andre returned to the table with a binder beneath his arm. It was thin, but I could sheets of paper sticking out from the small pile within. He slammed the binder down on the table. On the front of the binder was a taped label. On the label was written "Can You Move?"

I withheld laugh.

Lex was right.

"Um, Andre, what's this?" I asked without letting a single chuckle slip between my teeth.

"Our new game show," he said with such spirit that I had to let him continue. "It's a physical contest that will require the contestants to complete our exercises in time limits, faster than their competitors, or simply to last the longest in certain positions. Like, our box exercise could be a one-on-one contestant competition, or we could make it a tag team deal where the partners would have to work with two stacks of boxes. The first teammate would have to construct a new stack from the boxes of the tower they're deconstructing. The second teammate would deconstruct that tower to make their own. The first team to do that and the the reverse of that would be the winners. Oh, and the couch exercise would obviosuly be a team race. That's pretty self explanatory. The chair exercises would be to see who could hold their chair perpendicular to their arms the longest."

I wanted to laugh some more, but the ideas weren't half bad. He had a binder of notes, perhaps this could work out. He seemed to wanted it perfect before bringing it before me. The real question was, why was he bringing it to me. He had made connections through his moving company. He could've started this on his own. So, I asked him in a different, less confrontational way.

"Why haven't you tried to get this produced before? It sounds pretty good to me," I said. mY peripheral vision was still poorer than most people's, but I could see the silent surprise written all over Lex's face.

"I wanted to bring this to you first because you've done all the real research and you were the one who developed the exercises. I'd never take credit from you like that."

"Well, let me reward your loyalty with honesty," I told him as a warning. "I think this is a good idea, I do. But, it's not what I think would best get these exercises across the state, the country."

Andre took the blow harder than I expected, but his eyes grew much softer when Lex enclosed one of her hands around one of his. "You're the inventor. You decide."

"But I think you're on the right track," I said. "I think a televised segment of the exercises would be a good way to spread the word about it. And as for your title, with a little tweaking, we could have something."

His eyes brightened immediately. "You think so?"

"Yes, but this is going to take some time to nail down. We can't simply just ask a major tv network to allow us to come on to their sets so we can "move furniture around". This is a unique thing. We have to make people see it's uniqueness. Something about it has to charm people into wanting to do it, too."

"What things could we do to make it more likely to be accepted by the masses?"

"There are four things I know we'll need to do if we want it to be picked up. One- we'll need people to understand the ease of this type of workout compared to those at the gym. Two- we'll need a catchy name, one that's simple as Neptune Fitness, but with more a zip, a call to action. A name that will make people say, "Oh, I can do that it. It sounds like it'd be worth a shot. Three- we need to get funding. Without that, the first bullet point wouldn't be possible. Unless we get a sponsor, or a commercial deal, getting onto major television will be impossible. And four- we'll need an insignia."

"For the insignia, why not use your lion tattoo?" Lex asked.

"I would, but I want this to be something new. I don't want any part of my former life to co-exist with this vision."

"Why not use the tattoo you have hidden from us?" Andre suggested, pointing at the lump underneath my shirt. "I can still smell the faint traces of ink, and that looks an awful lot like the bandage they conceal fresh tattoos under."

I looked down at my breast, contemplating the logic of using a gladiator for a logo. After a few minutes, I had my answer. "I like the thought there, but I think it's too aggressive a picture. We're trying to go for simple tasks that can be repurposed as workouts. An insignia of a gladiator would kind of contradict that message since gladiators had a tendency to die in combat. We need something just as simple, but alluring. But let's not fret about it all right now. We'll take our time, we'll get it right, and we'll help people around the world learn to lose weight, even if it takes cities, one at a time, to do so."

CHAPTER 12
Right half of the board

And that, up until very recently, has been my life's story. It's not over. Not yet. Still plenty I'm hoping to achieve. Over the next year and a half, Lex, Andre and I worked painstakingly long to come to the terms of what I wanted my exercises to be. Nice, fun, affordable actions that anyone would be capable of. No need to squander your money at G.Y.M.s, or as I liked to call them, foundations where you G.ive Y.our M.oney away. I had no intentions of taking someone's hard earned money in exchange for their health. There was nothing noble about that. Well, unless you were a doctor, but they saved lives. I've never once heard from anyone I've known that the gym saved their life. They said they needed it, but not any longer. Not with my new exercise, which me and my partners dubbed "The Movement".

We've yet to adopt an insignia, but its hard to develop one for a loosely banded set of exercises as we had hammered out.

And yes, I am going to defy the hedonists assholes twisting things for their enjoyment. I still am. I'm alive. I'm kicking (back). And I'm on the losing side, at least for now.

I spent a good deal of time on their side, I realized one day. I remembered what Amber had said her main reason for wanting to divorce me was. I was dragging her around the world- quite literally- to service my whims, aspirations, and dreams. In return, I'd belittled hers so that she felt their was no true love between us. I was one of the hedonistic assholes. That's why they kept me alive. They saw I had the heart strings of a woman I could tug on. And I did.

But now, I wasn't that man. I was me. Jack Garbarino. I was going to stay me, this new, more bold, confident version of me. I was going to try and make something that could live beyond me.

Half my life was spent on the wrong half of the board. Now I was playing the half I needed to. I was going to make sure I ended my life on this side, just like Steve Jobs, Dende, and my parents. This gladiator was ready to make his mark.